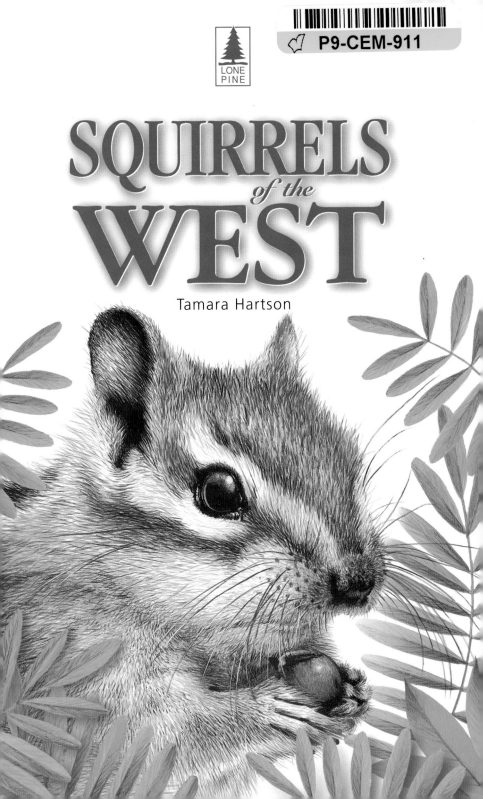

LONE PINE

SQUIRRELS
of the
WEST

Tamara Hartson

First Printed in 1999   10 9 8 7 6 5 4 3 2

Printed in Canada

The Publisher: Lone Pine Publishing

10145–81 Avenue   1808 B Street NW, Suite 140
Edmonton, AB T6E 1W9   Auburn, WA 98001
Canada   USA

Website: www.lonepinepublishing.com

Canada Cataloguing in Publication Data
Hartson, Tamara
    Squirrels of the west

    Includes bibliographical references and index.
    ISBN 1-55105-215-6

    1. Squirrels—Canada, Western—Identification. 2. Squirrels—West (U.S.)—
Identification. I. Title.
QL737.R68 H37 1999   599.36'09712   C99-910617-1

Editorial Director: Nancy Foulds
Project Editor: Roland Lines
Technical Review: Donald L. Pattie
Production Manager: Jody Reekie
Design & Production: Heather Markham
Cover Design: Rob Weidemann
Cover Illustration: Least Chipmunk by Gary Ross
Cartography: Jau-Ruey Marvin
Separations & Film: Elite Lithographers Company

All illustrations are by Gary Ross, except as follows: all track illustrations are by Ian Sheldon; the species illustrations on pages 37, 55, 97, 99 and 111 are by Kindrie Grove.

We acknowledge the financial support of the Government of Canada through the Book Publishing Industry Development Program (BPIDP) for our publishing activities.

PC: P4

Canada

CONTENTS

Richardson's Ground Squirrel

Reference Guide

Eastern Chipmunk
p. 14

Alpine Chipmunk
p. 16

Least Chipmunk
p. 18

Yellow-pine
Chipmunk, p. 20

Townsend's Chipmunk
p. 22

Yellow-cheeked
Chipmunk, p. 24

Allen's Chipmunk
p. 26

Siskiyou Chipmunk
p. 28

Sonoma Chipmunk
p. 30

Merriam's Chipmunk
p. 32

California Chipmunk
p. 34

Cliff Chipmunk
p. 36

Colorado Chipmunk
p. 38

Hopi Chipmunk
p. 40

Red-tailed
Chipmunk, p. 42

Gray-footed
Chipmunk, p. 44

Gray-collared
Chipmunk, p. 46

Reference Guide

| Long-eared Chipmunk, p. 48 | Lodgepole Chipmunk, p. 50 | Panamint Chipmunk, p. 52 | Uinta Chipmunk p. 54 | Palmer's Chipmunk p. 56 |

Alaska Marmot, p. 60   Woodchuck, p. 62   Yellow-bellied Marmot, p. 64

Hoary Marmot, p. 66   Olympic Marmot, p. 68   Vancouver Marmot, p. 70

| Harris's Antelope Squirrel, p. 74 | White-tailed Antelope Squirrel, p. 76 | Texas Antelope Squirrel, p. 78 | Nelson's Antelope Squirrel, p. 80 |

Reference Guide

Arctic Ground
Squirrel, p. 84

Columbian Ground
Squirrel, p. 86

Townsend's Ground
Squirrel, p. 88

Washington Ground
Squirrel, p. 90

Idaho Ground
Squirrel, p. 92

Richardson's Ground
Squirrel, p. 94

Wyoming Ground
Squirrel, p. 96

Uinta Ground
Squirrel, p. 98

Belding's Ground
Squirrel, p. 100

Thirteen-lined Ground
Squirrel, p. 102

Mexican Ground
Squirrel, p. 104

Spotted Ground
Squirrel, p. 106

Franklin's Ground
Squirrel, p. 108

Rock Squirrel
p. 110

California Ground
Squirrel
p. 112

Mohave Ground
Squirrel
p. 114

Round-tailed
Ground Squirrel
p.116

Golden-mantled
Ground Squirrel
p. 118

Cascade Golden-
mantled Ground
Squirrel, p. 120

Reference Guide

Black-tailed
Prairie-Dog, p. 124

White-tailed
Prairie-Dog, p. 126

Utah Prairie-
Dog, p. 128

Gunnison's
Prairie-Dog, p. 130

Eastern Gray
Squirrel, p. 134

Eastern Fox
Squirrel, p. 136

Mexican Fox
Squirrel, p. 138

Arizona Gray
Squirrel, p. 140

Western Gray
Squirrel, p. 142

Abert's Squirrel
p. 144

Red Squirrel
p. 146

Douglas's Squirrel
p. 148

Southern Flying
Squirrel, p. 152

Northern Flying
Squirrel, p. 154

7

Alpine Chipmunk

Introduction

I N THIS TIME WHEN MOST WILDLIFE IN NORTH AMERICA IS CONFINED TO NATIONAL parks and protected areas, we often overlook the wildness in our own backyards. Few animals have adapted to human urbanization, and of those that have, almost none are mammals. Most mammals are very sensitive to disturbance and habitat alteration, but many squirrel species live among our carefully pruned trees, eat from our routinely filled birdfeeders, benefit from our predator-reduced cities and then audaciously scold us for our trespasses. Such nerve! The squirrels' ability to thrive in our urban domain might be the reason that many people disregard and even disdain squirrels. If you look more closely at these fellow mammals, however, you will discover extremely sociable and familiar creatures. They are excellent builders, they are accomplished food gatherers, they work fervently to establish security for themselves in the face of inclemency, and they like to sleep late and lay in sunbeams.

The squirrels of the United States and Canada are quite diverse, ranging from ground-dwelling squirrels that live in tremendous underground colonies to flying squirrels that glide silently from tree to tree in the night. For those of us familiar with only a few neighborhood tree squirrels, a look at the diversity of the squirrel family can reveal bizarre adaptations, as well as some habits that are frequently considered, well, human. Not only are squirrels our distant kin, but when they occur in our backyards they are reminders of the wild environment that survives beyond our city limits.

Squirrels and Humans

While it is true that some squirrel species benefit from human activity, many species, especially the ground dwellers, have declined in number. Ground squirrels and prairie-dogs are often considered agricultural pests, and they were exterminated as vermin for many decades. Indeed, these little squirrels may eat seedling and ripe crops, but they usually also feed voraciously on insects that are damaging to crop plants. As well, the extensive burrowing of ground-dwelling squirrels serves to turn over and aerate the soil.

Another unfortunate effect of human activity on squirrels is the deforestation and fragmentation of primary tree squirrel habitat. Some tree squirrels, like the flying squirrels, are very sensitive to disturbance and competition from introduced species. Even something as simple as our pet cats can have a disastrous effect on the native squirrels of any region.

For centuries, many people have kept squirrels as pets. They are playful and inquisitive, and they are often reported as quick problem solvers (such as finding and opening food tins hidden high on kitchen shelves). Although squirrels can be interesting household pets, they do not litter train and must be considered as wild, not domestic, animals. Before acquiring a squirrel pet, remember that it has special needs and a wild nature—the placement of any wild animal in captivity has many ethical problems associated with it. Sadly, some squirrels that are raised as pets are later released into the wild, where they have no experience with food scarcity, harsh weather and predators.

Viewing Squirrels

Almost all kinds of squirrels are tolerant of humans, provided that we do not approach them too closely. Chipmunks can be viewed from just a few paces away as they sun themselves on rocks or clean their fur. Likewise, marmots and other ground dwellers will permit your unobtrusive presence as long as you are quiet and careful to avoid their burrow space. Tree squirrels are more difficult to view, simply because they are very active and, by comparison, we are too slow and awkward along the forest floor. To best view tree squirrels, pick a spot near a food source, such as a midden or even a birdfeeder, and watch them as they return faithfully every few minutes to deposit or collect food.

National parks and protected areas throughout North America are excellent places to view wildlife. Squirrels are not confined to these areas, but peaceful viewing of their daily activities is probably easiest there. Almost anywhere you go in the continent, whether to the mountains, the Arctic, the prairies or the desert, there is at least one squirrel species that will delight the quiet observer.

Sonoma Chipmunk

Squirrel Diversity

Squirrels belong to an order of mammals called rodents, which also includes voles, mice, beavers, pocket gophers and porcupines, and which is the largest and most diverse group of mammals in the world. Characteristically, rodents have two pairs of incisors—one pair on the upper jaw and the other on the lower jaw—and no canine teeth. The lack of canine teeth produces a gap, called the diastema, between the incisors and the molars. All rodent skulls can be identified by these features.

The squirrel family (Sciuridae), contains at least 273 species worldwide that show a great diversity in form and adaptation. All squirrels share common skull characteristics, but their outward appearances and behavioral characteristics are highly variable. North American squirrels can be broadly divided into two groups: the ground dwellers (five genera), which live in burrows, and the tree dwellers (three genera), which live in nests or cavities in trees. Most squirrels are active during the day, but others are nocturnal, and while many squirrels hibernate during winter or estivate during summer, some do not. Squirrels show very little sexual dimorphism, so that the males and females of a given species are similar in appearance. In most species the females are smaller, but female chipmunks tend to be larger and stronger than the males.

The evolution of squirrels dates back to at least the Late Oligocene period. The oldest fossils of ground-dwelling squirrels date back to the Upper Miocene period, approximately 12 million years ago. Tree squirrels, however, have fossil samples dating back to about 28 million years ago, indicating that the two groups branched off from each other early in their evolutionary history.

Six times as many squirrel species occur in western North America as in the East. Of the 66 squirrel species (from eight genera) in Canada and the United States, only 11 species are found east of the Mississippi. In the West, at least 65 squirrel species are found: 22 chipmunks, 6 marmots, 4 antelope squirrels, 19 ground squirrels, 4 prairie-dogs, 8 tree squirrels (from two genera) and 2 flying squirrels. This uneven distribution of squirrels on the continent may be the result of North America's Ice Ages, during which time squirrels and other animals were separated east to west; speciation on either side of the ice could have occurred at different rates.

Vancouver Marmot

About This Guide

Whether you are deep in the wilderness of a national park or simply watching the wildlife in your own backyard, keep this book handy to help you identify and understand each of the squirrel species you encounter.

This guide describes the 65 species of squirrels that are found west of the Mississippi River. The squirrels are presented in a generally accepted sequence that places the more closely related squirrels near one another. The scientific and common names used in this book, and the sequence of the groups (genera), follow the 'Revised checklist of North American mammals north of Mexico, 1997' (Jones et al. 1997). The sequence of species within each genus is based on *A Checklist of the Mammals of the World* (Hole 1995).

The quick reference guide, found on pages 4 to 7, illustrates all the squirrels in this book. It may help you identify the squirrel groups and species at a glance, and it leads you to the detailed descriptions of the squirrels.

Each group of squirrels is introduced with a brief description of its general characteristics. This introduction is not exhaustive, nor is it absolute. In almost every group there is at least one species that is nonconforming, a species that has unique and unusual traits. Often, these peculiar species are of special interest to observers. The track illustrations and burrow or nest layouts are, again, representative of the group. Every species, even individual squirrels within a species, will exhibit slightly different variations of the same basic plan.

The habitat in which you find a squirrel can often help you determine which species it is. A description of a species' habitat preference is part of each account; you can also use the habitat 'icons' that appear at the bottom of the second page as a fast reference to the species' preferred environments. The eight icons below are used in this book to represent generalized habitat types.

Before you finalize your decision on the species of a squirrel, check the 'similar species' section of the account; the species listed there are ones that could be mistakenly identified as the one you are considering. This section provides clues to help you differentiate among similar-looking squirrels, and it is usually accompanied by a small illustration of one of these other species.

Once you are familiar with the squirrels around you, enjoy them! They can be inquisitive and playful animals, and observing their antics can be a delightful experience.

Alpine/Arctic Tundra

Deserts

Rocky Slopes

Prairies or Meadows

Brushy Areas

Deciduous Forests

Coniferous Forests

Mixed Forests

Chipmunks

C hipmunks are probably the most amiable members of the squirrel family. Many children are introduced to chipmunks' striped backs and nut-loving ways in early childhood, and the appeal of the Chip and Dale caricatures may have built in us a special fondness for chipmunks. Regardless of the cute comics, however, few creatures are as endearing as a dark-eyed chipmunk sitting quietly on its hindfeet with its tiny 'hands' tucked close to its chest.

Most of the North American chipmunk species are very similar in appearance, and they are difficult to tell apart in the wild. The stripe pattern is consistent among chipmunks— five dark and four pales stripes down the back and alternating stripes on the face—but in some cases there are differences in coloration. There are also differences in the species' calls, which are highly variable, with most species using a combination of chirps, twitters, chatters and growls.

As ground dwellers, chipmunks usually nest in burrows or rock crevices. Some species have a tendency to nest in hollow tree limbs near the ground, and some individuals may even construct a tree nest. Unlike many other mammals, chipmunks are not strongly territorial over their home ranges. Tensions only rise when food stores or food sources are in danger of pilferage by other chipmunks.

The scientific name *Tamias* means 'storer,' and it refers to the food-hoarding habits of all chipmunks. Instead of relying on stored fat to survive winter, chipmunks generally fill their winter dens with immense amounts of food that they eat during wakeful periods of their hibernation. In chipmunks, the frequency of these wakeful periods is dependent primarily on latitude and climate, and only somewhat on species.

'work hole' (sealed up) *short side opening*

food cache

foreprint

hindprint

running trail

hibernating Yellow-pine Chipmunk

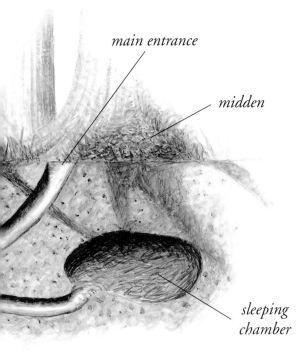

main entrance

midden

sleeping chamber

Eastern Chipmunk
(Chipping Squirrel)
Tamias striatus

Like its western counterparts, this common chipmunk of eastern North America has a striped back with five dark and four pale stripes. The two pale stripes on the sides are cream; the two pale stripes on the back are gray. This chipmunk occurs primarily in the East, but the western limit of its range extends from Manitoba to eastern Oklahoma. At one time, the Eastern Chipmunk was the sole member of the genus *Tamias*—all the western chipmunk species were previously classed in the genus *Eutamias*—but now biologists group all North American chipmunks in the genus *Tamias*.

The Eastern Chipmunk, which nests in an underground burrow, uses a tricky technique when creating its home. This chipmunk starts a 'work hole' to dig its burrow. After it finishes excavating the main passageway and sleeping chamber, the chipmunk seals up the work hole and opens a new entrance elsewhere. By excavating its burrow in this fashion, only the resident chipmunk knows the location of the tiny entranceway, which has no mound of dirt to disclose its whereabouts—all the excavated dirt is strewn outside the work hole.

ID: reddish-brown body; pale undersides; inner pale stripes are gray; outer pale stripes are cream colored and wider.

Size: *L* 8¹/₂–12 in (22–30 cm); *Wt* 2¹/₄–5 oz (64–142 g).

Habitat: deciduous woodlands; forest edges.

Nesting: burrows.

It is with a seemingly insatiable drive that the Eastern Chipmunk rapidly collects food for winter storage. When collecting berries, it runs along branches in the shrubs and quickly snips the stems of the berries with its sharp teeth. So speedy is its work that the ground beneath the bush is bombarded with a storm of berries. Once it has cut enough berries, the chipmunk scampers to the ground and carries the berries to a nearby cache. Most seeds, berries and nuts are collected in this manner, and the chipmunk eats these items during the wakeful periods of its hibernation.

SIMILAR SPECIES:
Least Chipmunk (p. 18) is smaller and its pale stripes are of equal width.

Least Chipmunk

outer pale stripes are
wide and cream colored

inner pale stripes are gray

underside is pale,
almost white

reddish-brown
body

Alpine Chipmunk

Tamias alpinus

A pale and tiny creature, the Alpine Chipmunk is at home in the high regions of the Sierra Nevada. Its coloration is lighter than most chipmunk species and slightly orangish in tone. Perhaps because of its extreme alpine habitat, the Alpine Chipmunk is one of the few chipmunk species to put on a layer of fat before entering hibernation, which lasts from mid-autumn to late spring. The fat layer greatly increases the chipmunk's chances of survival, as does the food stored in its den.

Adults usually emerge from their dens by June, refreshed and ready for courtship. Following several days of chase games and frolicking, the chipmunks mate. Once mating is complete, the individual chipmunks settle down and resume their solitary feeding and caching lifestyles. Females give birth to their litters in early summer, and the young grow rapidly for about five weeks. By six weeks, the youngsters have full-color coats and have almost achieved adult size.

ID: very small; yellow-gray coloration, often with orange tone on undersides, tail and face; clear, lightly contrasting stripes; outer dark stripes are rufous; central stripe is blackish; underside of tail is black edged and black tipped.

Size: L 6¹/₂–8 in (17–20 cm); Wt 1–1³/₄ oz (28–50 g).

Habitat: shale slopes; subalpine forests.

Nesting: burrows; rock crevices.

Alpine Chipmunks feed primarily on seeds and alpine plants, but they savor fungi and berries whenever possible. When Alpine Chipmunks are not feeding or storing food, they often spend warm afternoons sunbathing on rocks. They are very sensitive to high temperatures, however, and if the sun gets too warm they retreat to their nests. Chipmunks are comfortable only in fair weather: too much heat distresses them, and they cannot tolerate cold temperatures. If the day is stormy or even too windy, a chipmunk would rather stay warm in its den than go outside.

SIMILAR SPECIES:
Least Chipmunk (p. 18) has a longer tail and a yellowish, rather than orangish, coloration. All other chipmunks in the Sierra Nevada are larger and more darkly colored.

Least Chipmunk

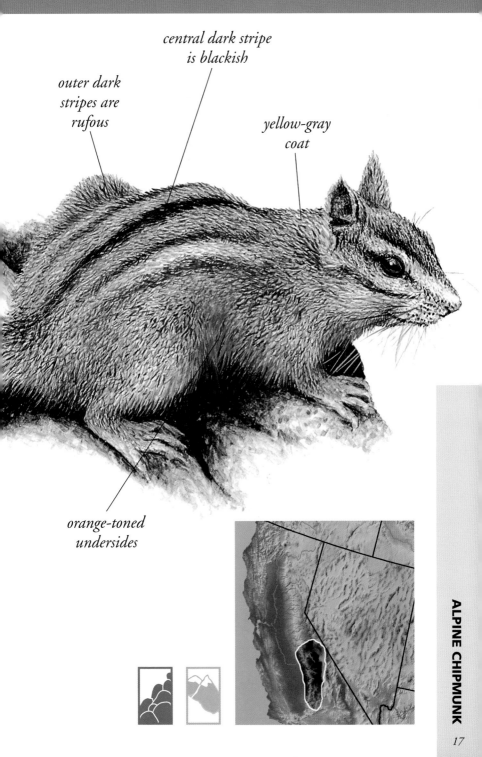

central dark stripe is blackish

outer dark stripes are rufous

yellow-gray coat

orange-toned undersides

Least Chipmunk

Tamias minimus

The five dark and four pale stripes down the back of a Least Chipmunk have a slightly gray tone to them, which distinguishes this chipmunk from the common Yellow-pine Chipmunk (p. 20). An adult Least Chipmunk has buffy-white undersides and a beige to rufous tail that is almost as long as its body. The Least Chipmunk undergoes two full molts each year, so its appearance changes seasonally, if only slightly: the summer coat is bright; the winter coat looks dusty.

Late in the summer, Least Chipmunks start to dig their winter burrows, which consist of one main passageway and one sleeping chamber. By November, their energetic food gathering stops and they start to spend more time in their burrows. Adults usually bed down first—youngsters must feed as late into the year as possible to catch up to the size and weight of the adults.

When Least Chipmunks hibernate, their periods of dormancy, which last from a couple of days to weeks at a time, are broken by wakeful periods during which they eat from their well-packed larders. The frequency of the wakeful periods depends on the latitude and climate of their home. Like many chipmunks, Least Chipmunks do not put on a layer of fat before hibernating, so they must eat frequently to survive winter.

ID: very small; muted to very bright colors; pale stripes are of equal width; pale undersides, with orange highlights; tail is light brown above, gray below.

Size: *L* 6⁵/₈–9 in (17–23 cm); *Wt* 1–1³/₄ oz (28–50 g).

Habitat: brushy areas; rocky outcroppings; forests.

Nesting: burrows; cavities in logs or trees.

SIMILAR SPECIES:
Alpine Chipmunk (p. 16) is found only in the Sierra Nevada and has a shorter tail. Hopi Chipmunk (p. 40) may be slightly larger and is generally more ochre colored. Most other chipmunks are larger.

Alpine Chipmunk

stripes have a gray cast and are equal in width

summer coat is brighter than winter coat

tail is beige or rufous and almost as long as body

tawny rump

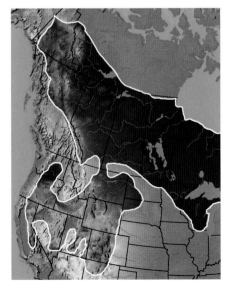

Yellow-pine Chipmunk

Tamias amoenus

A brightly colored animal, the Yellow-pine Chipmunk has distinct stripes and a luminous coat. It is often confused with the Least Chipmunk (p. 18), but a couple of good clues can help in distinguishing between the two: the overall color tone of the Yellow-pine Chipmunk's stripes is slightly orange, whereas the Least Chipmunk's stripes are slightly gray; and the Yellow-pine Chipmunk has an olive brown rump, in contrast to the tawny rump of the Least Chipmunk.

On warm days, Yellow-pine Chipmunks dart about looking for food. Their progress is erratic: they scamper short distances and then pause to look for danger. If a chipmunk senses something unusual or threatening, it calls out a shrill chatter, which warns any nearby chipmunks that a possible predator is in the area. When Yellow-pine Chipmunks are really scared, they hush up and run for cover.

Looking like kittens, hibernating Yellow-pine Chipmunks (see illustration, p. 12) curl up into tight balls and cover their eyes with their front paws. Once they are settled, their heart rate drops, their respiration slows, and their body temperature plummets. This condition is not easily reversible—a hibernating chipmunk takes many hours to come back to 'life' after it is disturbed. Normally, chipmunks wake approximately every two weeks to eat and rid their bodies of wastes. The exact frequency is dependent on the climate and latitude, and, when necessary, chipmunks may wake as often as every two days. Unlike ground squirrels, chipmunks typically do not have a fat layer, so they must eat to survive winter.

ID: richly colored, with tawny and orange highlights; stripes are distinct and of equal width; ears are dark in front, pale behind.

Size: *L* 7^1/$_4$–9^5/$_8$ in (18–24 cm); *Wt* 1–2^1/$_2$ oz (28–71 g).

Habitat: brushy areas of coniferous regions, especially yellow pine forests.

Nesting: burrows.

Lodgepole Chipmunk

SIMILAR SPECIES:
Least Chipmunk (p. 18) and Alpine Chipmunk (p. 16) are smaller and not as brightly colored. Uinta Chipmunk (p. 54) is darker and grayer. Lodgepole Chipmunk (p. 50) has stripes of varying width: the inner ones are narrow; the outer ones are wider.

ears are dark in front, paler toward rear

top of head is brown

stripes are distinct, with high contrast

orange highlights throughout coat

olive-brown rump

Townsend's Chipmunk

Tamias townsendii

The telltale flag of a Townsend's Chipmunk is its upright tail. Whether it's darting across hot stretches of beach sand or jumping through fern-shaded coastal forests, this chipmunk's tail advertises its whereabouts.

ID: very dark brown in color, with indistinct stripes; backs of ears are tawny on forepart, gray on hindpart; tail is grayish above, reddish below, and edged with white-tipped hairs.

Size: *L* 8¹/₂–14 in (22–36 cm); *Wt* 1³/₄–4 oz (50–113 g).

Habitat: humid forests, both hardwood and coniferous.

Nesting: burrows.

Large and strong, the Townsend's Chipmunk is an excellent climber and avid explorer. It is known to travel for more than half a mile (800 m) in search of food, which can be seeds, roots, bulbs, green plants, large insects or even birds' eggs and fledglings. With cheek pouches that can hold more than 100 oats, it is able to transport large quantities of food to its larder. In the northern limits of its range, the Townsend's Chipmunk hibernates throughout the winter; in mild southern climates, it tends to remain active all year.

Few chipmunks outweigh the darkly colored Townsend's Chipmunk. Females are largest—they top the scales at nearly 4 oz (110 g)—and newborn Townsend's Chipmunks are the largest chipmunk babies. Townsend's Chipmunks are usually solitary, but they can be locally abundant and give the appearance of a colony in some areas. Each chipmunk is far too concerned with gathering food for itself, however, to worry about home territories or trespassers.

Until recently, three other chipmunks—the Allen's (p. 26), Siskiyou (p. 28) and Yellow-cheeked (p. 24) chipmunks—were thought to be part of the Townsend's Chipmunk species. All four chipmunks are outwardly very similar—they are distinguished from one another based on subtle differences in their calls and the structure of the penis bone—but they do not interbreed, even in areas where their ranges overlap.

SIMILAR SPECIES:
Sonoma Chipmunk (p. 30) has solid-colored ears. Long-eared Chipmunk (p. 48) has distinct white patches behind the ears. Yellow-cheeked Chipmunk (p. 24) has a less-bushy tail and is darker in color. Allen's Chipmunk (p. 26) and Siskiyou Chipmunk (p. 28) differ from the Townsend's primarily in call and range, but the Allen's may appear larger in fall, and the Siskiyou may appear darker in color.

Sonoma Chipmunk

indistinct stripes

bicolored ears

tail is grayish above, reddish below and edged with white-tipped hairs

dark brown coloration

Yellow-cheeked Chipmunk

Tamias ochrogenys

For a chipmunk enthusiast, spotting a Yellow-cheeked Chipmunk is quite an achievement. These elusive chipmunks live deep in the forests of north-coastal California, where they are more often heard than seen. Like ventriloquists, their metallic chatters can be heard clearly amidst the trees, but the source cannot be pinpointed.

This stripy beast is among the largest of chipmunks, about the same size as the closely related Townsend's Chipmunk (p. 22). The Yellow-cheeked Chipmunk has the longest head and body of all its western relatives. With its long, streamlined body, this chipmunk is a fluid and agile climber.

Among the redwoods of its home ground, Yellow-cheeked Chipmunks eat a wide range of seeds, nuts, berries and mushrooms. A typical chipmunk day is spent either energetically collecting and storing food or lounging in sunbeams. Sunbathing is a favorite pastime of many chipmunks, and they will frequently stretch out on warm sand or rocks to absorb the heat.

Whether resting or feeding, chipmunks always keep an eye out for danger. Even the shadow of a raptor flying overhead is enough to alert these chipmunks and send them scurrying to safety. As it scampers away, a frightened chipmunk calls out a series of *chik, chik, chik* sounds to warn any nearby chipmunks of the lurking danger. Hawks, foxes, snakes and weasels are the main predators of Yellow-cheeked Chipmunks. Despite being the targets of such cunning animals, chipmunks have unusual longevity and may live for five to eight years in the wild.

ID: large chipmunk; dark coloration is rich brown; central stripe is darkest and most prominent of dark stripes; distinct pale patches behind ears; lower facial stripe is tawny brown.

Size: *L* 9¼–12 in (24–30 cm); *Wt* 2⅛–4¼ oz (60–120 g).

Habitat: coastal redwood forests.

Nesting: burrows.

SIMILAR SPECIES:
Townsend's (p. 22), Allen's (p. 26) and Siskiyou (p. 28) chipmunks have bushy tails and less distinct stripes. Merriam's Chipmunk (p. 32) and Sonoma Chipmunk (p. 30) are smaller.

Siskiyou Chipmunk

dorsal stripe is darkest and most prominent

pale patches behind ears

lower facial stripe is tawny brown

rich brown coloration

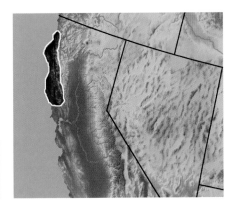

Allen's Chipmunk

Tamias senex

The Allen's Chipmunk and the Lodgepole Chipmunk (p. 50) share an inordinate fondness for eating fungi. Little craters can be found throughout areas inhabited by these chipmunks, indicating where a truffle or other fungus was dug up.

ID: large, grayish chipmunk; stripes are usually indistinct, except for central dark stripe; prominent white spots behind ears; tail is pale tawny with light edges.

Size: L 9–10 in (23–25 cm); Wt 2¹/₂–3⁷/₈ oz (71–110 g).

Habitat: dense, humid fir forests.

Nesting: burrows.

The variable pelage of the Allen's Chipmunk—its coat color and contrast changes both seasonally and regionally—makes visual identification of this species difficult. The best ways to identify an Allen's Chipmunk are by habitat, call and the holes it makes in the ground to get at fungi. Different from every other species, the Allen's Chipmunk calls out three to five metallic barks, followed by a single chirped note, in forests of white or red fir and humid, lush, brushy areas—its favored habitats.

The Allen's Chipmunk is one of the few species of chipmunks in North America to put on a layer of fat to survive the winter months. Increasing their weight by as much as 20 percent before November, Allen's Chipmunks wake less frequently from hibernation than other chipmunks, and their first incidence of wakefulness is delayed. The majority of chipmunks rely solely on the food they have piled up in their winter dens, waking at intervals to eat a large meal from their well-stocked pantries. Allen's Chipmunks have both a fat layer and a larder to feed from during the few wakeful periods of their hibernation.

In mid-March, the number of Allen's Chipmunks running about the twigs and underbrush of central Oregon and northern California starts to increase as their hibernation comes to an end. The chipmunks remain active from late April to early November, but only during daylight hours. Throughout November, the number of active Allen's Chipmunks dwindles again, indicating the beginning of hibernation.

SIMILAR SPECIES:
Yellow-cheeked Chipmunk (p. 24) is darker and has more distinct stripes. Townsend's Chipmunk (p. 22), which looks almost identical, does not sound a chirped note after a series of barks. Siskiyou Chipmunk (p. 28) is slightly darker, but not as dark as the Yellow-cheeked.

Yellow-cheeked Chipmunk

highly variable coat
color (may appear very
gray in some regions)

whitish patches
behind ears

indistinct stripes

tail is tawny in color,
with light-colored edges

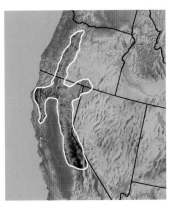

Siskiyou Chipmunk

Tamias siskiyou

This chipmunk is a member of a closely related group of four chipmunk species—the Siskiyou, Townsend's (p. 22), Yellow-cheeked (p. 24) and Allen's (p. 26) chipmunks were once considered the same species. All four of these large chipmunks have similar outward appearances; their distinguishing characteristics occur in their calls, certain bone structures and specific ecological niches. Where two or more of these species occur together, they maintain separate habitats and do not interbreed. The Siskiyou Chipmunk is named for the Siskiyou Mountains of Oregon and California, which is its primary range.

Like most chipmunks, the Siskiyou Chipmunk prefers a solitary lifestyle. Social interactions between chipmunks are rare and short lived. In spring, males are energetic and looking for receptive females. Courtship involves playful games of tag where two or even three chipmunks dart through the underbrush. As is true in the courtship of many mammal species, a certain level of propriety is necessary if mating between the chipmunks is to occur: ill-mannered males who act inappropriately once in the burrow may end up getting walloped and tossed out by the slightly larger females.

After the breeding season, males and females have very little to do with each other. Following 30 or 31 days of gestation, the female has a litter of three to five pups. The young are born blind and helpless, looking more like pink Gummy Bears than real animals. These tiny babies have impressive growth rates, however, and after just five weeks they are almost full grown and have full-color coats. Youngsters are high-spirited, and they attack each other with vigor. The mother is also energetic and often takes them out in the evening for wrestling matches in the grass and games of 'follow-the-leader.' Exhausted, the little ones fall fast asleep when they return home.

ID: large chipmunk; dark dorsal stripes are nearly black; inner pale stripes may be pinkish or cinnamon; outer pale stripes are light gray; ears may be tawny in front, gray behind; tail is reddish, sometimes with white edge.

Size: *L* 8¹/₂–11 in (22–28 cm); *Wt* 1³/₄–4 oz (50–113 g).

Habitat: brushy areas to open forests.

Nesting: burrows.

SIMILAR SPECIES:
Townsend's Chipmunk (p. 22) does not have black stripes all year. Allen's Chipmunk (p. 26) is paler. Yellow-cheeked Chipmunk (p. 24) is darker and usually browner, rather than with black or gray tones.

Townsend's Chipmunk

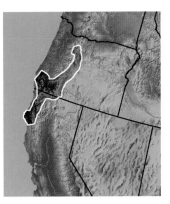

reddish tail

inner pair of pale stripes
may have pinkish or
cinnamon highlights

dark stripes are
nearly black

outer pale stripes
are light gray

Sonoma Chipmunk

Tamias sonomae

When many species of chipmunks occupy the same geographic range, they frequently develop differences between their calls, which allows each chipmunk to identify members of its own species. The Sonoma Chipmunk lives in northwestern California, where several other chipmunk species also dwell, and its call is slower and lower in pitch than the calls of other chipmunks.

Sonoma Chipmunks spend great lengths of time stretched out on logs or the tops of bushes, where they partake of warm sunbeams and a view of their surroundings. When they are not basking, they are eagerly searching for food and stuffing their larders. Their coats are tinged dark brown, and the outer pair of dark stripes are often indistinct, a common trait among chipmunks of the Pacific Northwest. The pale stripes on the Sonoma Chipmunk appear slightly yellow.

Mating occurs in early spring. After a gestation period of about 30 days, the female gives birth to four or five blind, helpless and very hungry babies. The tiny babies are born in their mother's hibernation den, but she may move them elsewhere as the weather improves. After five weeks of care, the young have striped coats like their mother and are almost as big. Once out of the nest, the youngsters stay with their mother for up to three weeks, playing games of tag, wrestling and learning some essential skills that will help them survive on their own. The mother leaves when she decides her young are ready for independence, but the siblings might stay together for several weeks longer. Eventually, they all split up and start their own burrows.

ID: large, brown chipmunk; outermost pair of dark stripes are indistinct; no black in facial stripes; dark spots between ear and eye; tail is reddish, paler at base.

Size: *L* 8¹/₂–11 in (22–28 cm); *Wt* 1³/₄–3³/₄ oz (50–106 g).

Habitat: brushy and open areas of coniferous forests.

Nesting: burrows.

SIMILAR SPECIES:
Yellow-cheeked Chipmunk (p. 24) is less tawny and has less distinct stripes. Townsend's (p. 22), Allen's (p. 26) and Siskiyou (p. 28) chipmunks are all darker.

Yellow-cheeked Chipmunk

pale stripes appear
slightly yellow

facial stripes are
brown, with no black
in them

tail is reddish,
paler at base

coat is mainly brown

outermost dark stripes
are indistinct

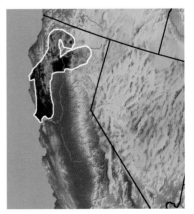

Merriam's Chipmunk

Tamias merriami

Like all chipmunks, the Merriam's Chipmunk has nine stripes running the length of its body, from head to tail: one dark stripe down the center of its back, two dark stripes on each side of its face and body and four pale stripes between the dark stripes. The Merriam's Chipmunk lives in southern and central California, and it shares many characteristics with other western chipmunks, making proper identification in the wild a difficult task. The overall coloration of a Merriam's Chipmunk is often blurry and lacks intensity, as if it took a dunk in a mud puddle.

ID: grayish-brown overall; indistinct stripes; white undersides; small, dark spots in front of and behind eyes; tail is edged with fine white hairs.

Size: L 8¹/₄–11 in (21–28 cm); Wt 2¹/₂–4 oz (71–113 g).

Habitat: rocky, shrubby areas; upper edge of chaparral.

Nesting: burrows.

Merriam's Chipmunks favor coniferous and rocky habitats in mountain regions. Food is abundant for them in their low mountain homes, and their favorite meals include piñon pine nuts, acorns, flowers and fruits. Throughout summer, adults collect tremendous amounts of seeds and nuts, most of which they store for winter use. These chipmunks do not put on a layer of fat to survive through winter, and during hibernation they wake periodically to feed from their larders.

Unwitting forest helpers, chipmunks are vital components of a forest ecosystem: the extensive burrows they dig aerate the soil and bring up earth from below; their feeding habits help keep in check many weed and insect species that are prone to population outbursts; their forgotten seed caches germinate, augmenting seed dispersal for forest plants; and they are an essential prey species for many forest carnivores.

SIMILAR SPECIES:
Long-eared Chipmunk (p. 48) has a distinct white patch behind each ear. California Chipmunk (p. 34) is paler and less brightly colored. All other chipmunks in the same range have distinct stripes.

Long-eared Chipmunk

stripes are indistinct

undersides are white

tail is often edged with fine white hairs

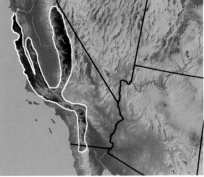

California Chipmunk

Tamias obscurus

Many of the chipmunks look almost identical, but several species have peculiar behavioral characteristics that help distinguish them from the others. California Chipmunks are selective about where they call from: they will not call while sitting in a tree, only from the tops of bushes. The vocal repertoire of these chipmunks is highly varied, including sharp barks, chirps, *chik*s and *chuck-a-chuck*s. Certain types of calls serve as warnings to nearby chipmunks when a predator is spotted. The *chuck* sound, for example, causes other chipmunks close by to be quiet and alert. Other calls are more sociable and encourage neighboring chipmunks to join in a conversation.

California Chipmunks typically live in burrows in the ground. They are underground architects, designing pockets in their main tunnel for either turning around or for storing waste. The den space in their burrow is large enough to contain stored food. Although chipmunks have large stores of food in their winter dens, they still make many caches of food separate from their main larder. Caches speckled around the vicinity of their burrow vary in size and food type: in one spot a chipmunk might bury four or five nuts; close by there might be a cache of 200 oats. Using primarily their sense of smell, the chipmunk later returns to its caches to dig up the goods. Sometimes caches are forgotten, especially if the food has very little odor, such as some seeds and nuts. Forgotten seed caches may sprout and give rise to new plants. By this process, chipmunks are important agents of distribution for plant species.

ID: top of head is pale gray; brown facial stripes; black eye stripe; indistinct dorsal stripes; reddish dark stripes; grayish pale stripes.

Size: *L* 8 1/4–9 1/4 in (21–24 cm); *Wt* 2–3 1/4 oz (57–92 g).

Habitat: deciduous and coniferous forests with rocky outcroppings.

Nesting: burrows.

SIMILAR SPECIES:
Merriam's Chipmunk (p. 32) also has indistinct stripes, but with less-reddish dark stripes.

Merriam's Chipmunk

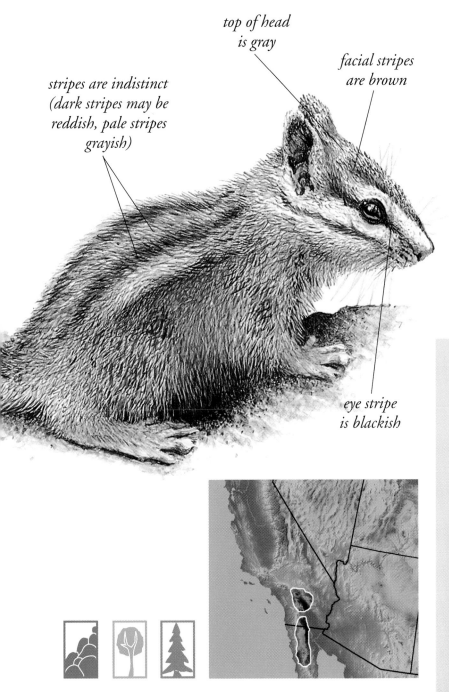

top of head
is gray

facial stripes
are brown

stripes are indistinct
(dark stripes may be
reddish, pale stripes
grayish)

eye stripe
is blackish

Cliff Chipmunk

Tamias dorsalis

With noticeable gray throughout its coat, the Cliff Chipmunk is fairly easy to identify. The alternating dark and light stripes down its back are black and gray, rather than the black and cream-colored stripes of other chipmunks. During winter, the Cliff Chipmunk's coat can be so gray and dusty that the stripes down its back are indistinguishable.

Throughout most of its range, the Cliff Chipmunk hibernates during the winter months. It is only in Arizona, where winters are mild enough, that this chipmunk is able to remain active all year. True to its name, the Cliff Chipmunk prefers to den in rocky outcroppings or cliffs. Areas where the rocks are topped with brushy plants provide ideal habitat, because these chipmunk benefit from the safety of camouflage among twigs and shadows. Deep rock crevices beneath the shrubs make suitable and safe homes for these agile climbers.

Unlike their solitary cousins, Cliff Chipmunks will sometimes collect in groups to feed when food is plentiful. The groups are mostly female, contain about 10 chipmunks each, and keep their distance from each other. Chipmunks have exceptional manual dexterity, which enables them to eat many items that would otherwise be unmanageable for such diminutive creatures—their paws are nearly a blur as they rotate large berries and nuts until they find a good tooth-hold. With their nimble teeth, chipmunks can separate seeds from husks in one quick movement.

ID: indistinct stripes on grayish body; clearer facial stripes; bushy tail is rufous colored underneath.

Size: *L* 7¹/₂–11 in (19–28 cm); *Wt* 2–3 oz (57–85 g).

Habitat: piñon pine and juniper slopes; forest edges; cliffs and rocky areas.

Nesting: burrows; rock crevices.

California Chipmunk

SIMILAR SPECIES:
California Chipmunk (p. 34) and Merriam's Chipmunk (p. 32) also have indistinct stripes, but they both occur further west, in California.

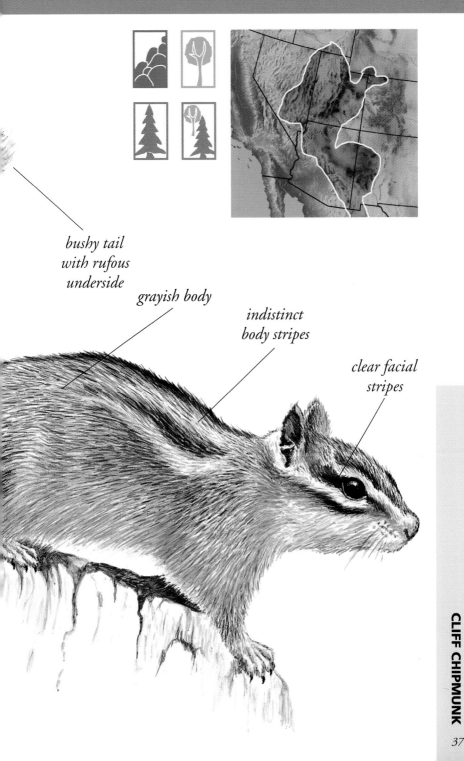

bushy tail
with rufous
underside

grayish body

indistinct
body stripes

clear facial
stripes

Colorado Chipmunk

Tamias quadrivittatus

An abundant resident of Utah, Colorado, Arizona and New Mexico, the Colorado Chipmunk inhabits a variety of different habitats, including desert scrub, tundra, grassland-chaparral and coniferous forests. It is an agile climber, and it is more at home in trees than the other shrub-loving chipmunks. Its sharp claws and dauntless nature give it access to almost any food source, including conifer cones, nuts, seeds, insects, snails, fungi and birds' eggs. The Colorado Chipmunk is a connoisseur of spruce cones, and it will fearlessly climb to the tops of spruce trees to dine on these choice meals.

ID: orange to brownish overall; creamy undersides; 3 inner dark stripes are black; outermost stripes are brown; tail is white edged and black tipped; ears are blackish in front, whitish behind.

Size: L 8¹/₄–9¹/₂ in (21–24 cm); Wt 2–3 oz (57–85 g).

Habitat: various, from desert scrub to tundra and coniferous forests.

Nesting: mainly burrows; possibly tree cavities.

Throughout the long summers of the southern states, Colorado Chipmunks leisurely gather food and pack their larders. They are usually active from late February to mid-November—these chipmunks spend less time hibernating than most other western species. In winter months, they eat from their food caches during wakeful periods of their dormancy. They also use the stored food during summer if they are confined to their burrows by bad weather.

The medium-sized Colorado Chipmunk generally has an orange glow about its coat, except on the shoulders, which are gray, and the tail, which is black tipped and white bordered.

When startled, a Colorado Chipmunk issues a sharp warning bark and darts for cover—a quick retreat is essential for the survival of such diminutive creatures ill suited to self-defense. The escape technique proves successful, resulting in an exceptional longevity of six or seven years for these small rodents.

Uinta Chipmunk

SIMILAR SPECIES:
Uinta Chipmunk (p. 54) appears brownish. Hopi Chipmunk (p. 40) is smaller, paler and generally reddish in appearance.

ears are dark in front, paler toward rear

black-tipped tail

tail is fringed with white

inner three dark stripes are almost black

Hopi Chipmunk

Tamias rufus

The Hopi Chipmunk is easily confused with both the Colorado Chipmunk (p. 38) and the Least Chipmunk (p. 18). In fact, the Hopi Chipmunk was only recently designated a separate species from the Colorado Chipmunk, based on evidence that the two do not interbreed where their ranges overlap. The only visual clue to help distinguish between the two is that the Hopi Chipmunk is usually darker and more reddish in color. The Least Chipmunk tends to hold its tail more upright than does the Hopi Chipmunk.

Inhabiting a small range in northern Arizona, western Colorado and eastern Utah, the Hopi Chipmunk lives in coniferous rocky areas with lots of juniper shrubs. Hopi Chipmunks feed on grasses, conifers seeds and green vegetation, but they have a particular fondness for the cones of one-seeded juniper. Like others of their kind, Hopi Chipmunks zealously collect cones and seeds and stash them away for winter use.

The constant hoarding of food by chipmunks is not without explanation: food hoarded by a chipmunk throughout summer becomes vital to its survival in winter. When they hibernate, chipmunks do not enter a long-term dormancy and live off their body fat like marmots. Instead, chipmunks have intermittent wakeful periods during which they feed and rid their bodies of wastes. Depending on the latitude and climate of a chipmunk's home, its dormant periods may last from a few days to a couple of weeks. If a chipmunk were to wake and find its caches empty, starvation would be imminent. Hopi Chipmunks do not hibernate for as long as some of the more northern chipmunks, but they will spend at least from November to late February in their winter dens.

ID: generally ochre colored; dark stripes are reddish brown, without any black; outer set of dark stripes are very faint; distinct white patch behind ears; tail is dark chestnut above, tawny below.

Size: L 6⅝–9 in (17–23 cm); Wt 1½–2 oz (43–57 g).

Habitat: rocky outcroppings with juniper; brushy areas; piñon pine forests.

Nesting: burrows; rock crevices.

SIMILAR SPECIES:
Least Chipmunk (p. 18) is usually smaller and carries its tail more upright. Colorado Chipmunk (p. 38) is larger and brighter in color, with more contrast between the dark and light stripes.

Least Chipmunk

tail is
chsestnut
above, tawny
below

outer dark stripes
are very faint

dark stripes are
reddish brown

distinct white patch
behind ears

Red-tailed Chipmunk

Tamias ruficaudus

True to its name, the Red-tailed Chipmunk has a distinctly rust-colored tail. White undersides, cinnamon feet and an olive brown rump also help distinguish this species from other chipmunks.

Skillful climbers, these rufous-shaded chipmunks prefer to live in dense coniferous forests, where they partake in both terrestrial and arboreal lifestyles, nesting either in a tree or on the ground. A typical tree nest looks like a shaggy ball of grass and leaves, 20–60 ft (6–18 m) off the ground. Treetop architects, these chipmunks design their tree nests to be hollow and roomy inside and about 12–16 in (30–40 cm) in diameter. Ground nests can be found in stumps, under logs or in burrows. To make the ground nests comfortable, these chipmunks line their den chambers with dry grass and leaves.

Cranberries, honeysuckles, black locusts and fir seeds are among the preferred foods of the Red-tailed Chipmunk. Over summer, chipmunks store large quantities of food in both their main dens and in small caches. At the end of summer, any food remaining in the caches is transferred to the winter chamber. Seed caches that are forgotten may germinate the following season, thus helping to renew the plants on which the chipmunks feed. Like sleeping in a refrigerator, a chipmunk curls up in its cool winter den surrounded by piles of food. Such large quantities of food are necessary because chipmunks do not put on a layer of fat to survive the winter; instead, they wake frequently from hibernation to eat.

ID: large chipmunk; tawny overall, with contrasting gray rump; 3 inner dark stripes are black; outermost stripes are brown; rufous tail.

Size: *L* 8³/₄–9³/₄ in (22–25 cm); *Wt* 2–2¹/₂ oz (57–71 g).

Habitat: coniferous forests; rocky outcroppings.

Nesting: burrows; leafy tree nests.

SIMILAR SPECIES:
Least Chipmunk (p. 18) is smaller. Yellow-pine Chipmunk (p. 20) has a yellowish underside of the tail.

Yellow-pine Chipmunk

reddish or rufous tail

cinnamon-colored
feet

gray rump

inner three
dark stripes
are black

Gray-footed Chipmunk

Tamias canipes

Although most chipmunks appear similar at first glance, the Gray-footed Chipmunk, as its name suggests, is the only species that consistently has gray on the top sides of its hindfeet. The rest of the Gray-footed Chipmunk's coat is not so consistent, however, and it shows a slight color variation throughout its range. Gray-foots living in old lava fields in New Mexico, for example, have generally darker coats—the dark pelage gives them better camouflage against the dark lava rock.

The Gray-footed Chipmunk diligently collects a large variety of fruits, nuts and seeds, which it stores away in numerous food caches. The persistence with which a chipmunk hoards food is admirable: if it comes across a buffet of choice foods, such as a campsite or birdfeeder, it will energetically fill its cheeks and start carrying load after load to some secluded cache. After it has carted away the bulk of the goods, it may finally eat some. Even after a big meal, this industrious gatherer gets right back to work.

When they are not storing food for winter, Gray-footed Chipmunks are either sunbathing or grooming. Chipmunks frequently lie on rocks or stretch out in the tops of bushes to warm themselves in the sun. They cannot tolerate extreme heat, however, and when they get too hot they must retire to their burrows. Grooming is part of their daily routine; they use their paws to clean off their fur, and then they lick their paws clean, too. Chipmunks will roll in dust on occasion to remove any mites and ticks that have accumulated in their fur.

ID: small chipmunk; grayish cast to fur; distinct stripes; dark stripes are brown; pale stripes are whitish; nape, shoulders and tops of hindfeet are gray.

Size: L 8¼–11 in (21–28 cm); Wt 2–3 oz (57–85 g).

Habitat: forested areas, especially coniferous forests; rocky areas; brushy hillsides.

Nesting: burrows; log cavities.

SIMILAR SPECIES:
Gray-collared Chipmunk (p. 46) is darker overall and has a gray 'collar.' Colorado Chipmunk (p. 38) has a tawny appearance.

Gray-collared Chipmunk

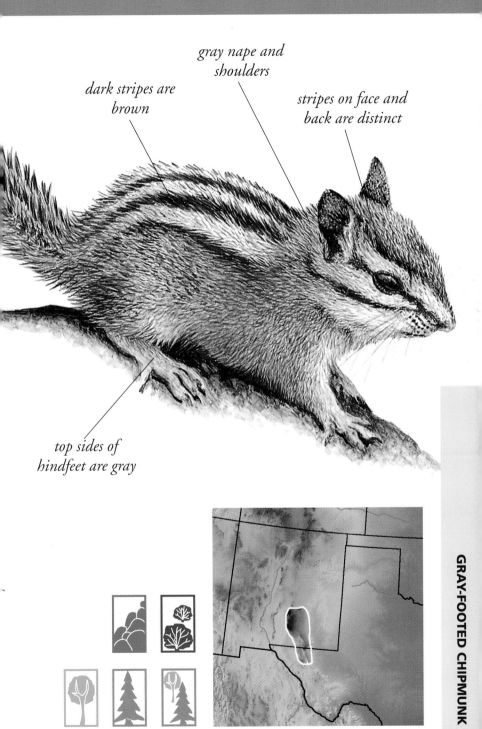

gray nape and shoulders

dark stripes are brown

stripes on face and back are distinct

top sides of hindfeet are gray

Gray-collared Chipmunk
(Gray-necked Chipmunk)
Tamias cinereicollis

The Gray-collared Chipmunk's name refers to the grayish fur on its upper back and shoulders. An even better clue to its identity, however, is its cheek color—this chipmunk is the only species with consistently gray cheeks. As well, the fur of its tail is predominantly gray.

A good climber, the Gray-collared Chipmunk likes dense foliage and tree cover—its primary range is in the ponderosa pine and spruce forests of east-central Arizona and southwestern New Mexico. Because it lives in such a mild climate, this chipmunk may not hibernate, but it still stashes food throughout summer and feeds from its caches during winter, when fresh food is scarce.

In spring, males eagerly set off to look for mates. In June, females will bear a litter of four to seven young after about 30 days of gestation. The mother usually gives birth in her burrow, but she will transfer her babies one by one to a tree nest when the weather warms up. The babies, though helpless at first, grow very quickly. When the young are five weeks old they are weaned, but they continue to live with their mother. Youngsters are playful, attacking each other in mock combat. Their play fighting and games of chase build strength and dexterity. Throughout summer, the mother joins in the games with her youngsters and also takes them on field trips to learn about the world. In fall, the young are ready to disperse from their mother and start their own burrows. If they survive their first winter, they have good chances of raising their own families and living for up to five years.

ID: dark gray back and head; light gray neck and shoulders; pale gray undersides; distinctly gray cheeks; stripes are usually distinct, except for outer-most dark stripes.

Size: *L* 8¼–10 in (21–25 cm); *Wt* 2–3 oz (57–85 g).

Habitat: open ponderosa pine and spruce forests.

Nesting: burrows; tree nests.

SIMILAR SPECIES:
Least Chipmunk (p. 18) and Gray-footed Chipmunk (p. 44) lack the gray 'collar,' and the Gray-footed has browner stripes and paler sides. No other chipmunk has gray cheeks. All other chipmunks in the same range have indistinct stripes.

Gray-footed Chipmunk

predominantly
gray tail

light gray neck
and shoulders

stripes are
usually distinct

dark gray
head

pale gray
undersides

Long-eared Chipmunk

Tamias quadrimaculatus

The presence of Long-eared Chipmunks in the Sierra Nevada of northeastern California is made obvious by torn-apart conifer cones and tiny craters in the ground. Long-eared Chipmunks have a predilection for eating fungi, and they frequently dig up tasty mushrooms and truffles, in addition to their regular diet of seeds, nuts, caterpillars, beetle larvae and termites.

Long-eared Chipmunks must eat the fresh grubs and fungi while they can; when they retire for hibernation in late November, they must rely on their larder of stored seeds and nuts. Long-eared Chipmunks are light hibernators, and they wake every few days to eat a good meal and rid their bodies of wastes. On particularly nice winter days, a few chipmunks may venture out of their burrows to play before starting the next period of hibernation.

In spring, the males usually emerge from hibernation before the females. Courtship and mating may occur anytime between April and June. After mating, the chipmunks have little to do with each other. Following a gestation period of about 31 days, the female gives birth to a litter of two to six young. Like all other chipmunks, Long-eared Chipmunks start life looking like red-and-pink jellybeans; within five weeks they transform into fully striped young adults.

Despite its name, there is not a readily visible difference in ear length between the Long-eared Chipmunk and the other species. Mature Long-eared Chipmunks, however, do have prominent patches of white behind each ear—these patches are much larger than those on other species.

ID: large chipmunk; overall reddish tinge and bright colors; little contrast between light and dark stripes; reddish tail is edged with white.

Size: *L* 7³/₄–10 in (20–25 cm); *Wt* 2¹/₂–3¹/₂ oz (71–99 g).

Habitat: open brushy areas; coniferous forests.

Nesting: burrows.

Merriam's Chipmunk

SIMILAR SPECIES:
Townsend's Chipmunk (p. 22) and Merriam's Chipmunk (p. 32) have a brown stripe below the ear. Most other chipmunks in the same range are smaller and have indistinct stripes.

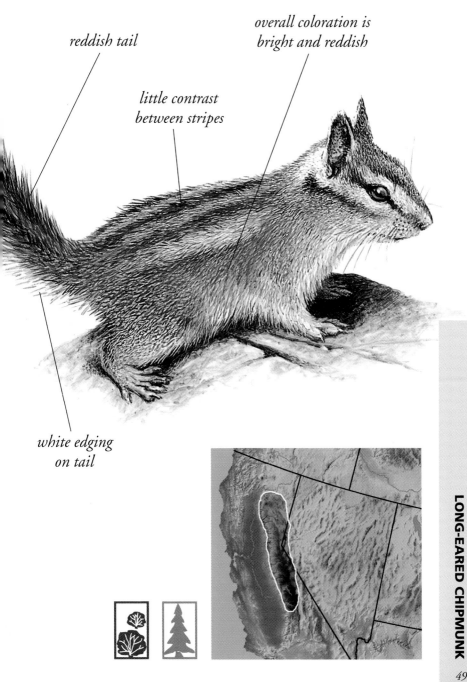

reddish tail

overall coloration is
bright and reddish

little contrast
between stripes

white edging
on tail

Lodgepole Chipmunk

Tamias speciosus

Appropriately enough, the Lodgepole Chipmunk is commonly associated with lodgepole pine and red fir forests in the mountains of eastern and central California. It shares much of this range with the Merriam's Chipmunk (p. 32), which is the low-elevation counterpart to the Lodgepole Chipmunk. The separation of chipmunk species into specialized niches, whether by habitat type, elevation or other preferences, is what allows more than one species to thrive in the same geographic range.

Seeds and nuts are the standard fare for all chipmunks, but each chipmunk species may dine on one delicacy all to themselves. The favorite food of the Lodgepole Chipmunk is subterranean fungi, and a Lodgepole Chipmunk's home territory will be pitted with excavation sites.

Although chipmunks primarily feed on plant material, most of them have mildly predaceous tendencies. Throughout summer, when fresh food is abundant, Lodgepole Chipmunks may chase and eat a variety of small animals; insects are almost a staple for some chipmunks. Chipmunks are not usually finicky eaters, but they eat insects in a very particular fashion: they gingerly toss away the head and legs to savor the tender abdomen. As well as insects, Lodgepole Chipmunks eat snails, slugs, birds' eggs, fledglings, small mice and young frogs. There is even a record of one chipmunk that caught and ate a 2-ft (60-cm) garter snake!

ID: stripes are distinct, but with little contrast between light and dark stripes; outermost dark stripes may be nonexistent; muted facial stripes; ears are dark in front, light behind; dark spots in front of and behind eyes; tail may have dark ring near tip.

Size: *L* 7³/₄–9¹/₂ in (20–24 cm); *Wt* 1³/₄–2¹/₈ oz (50–60 g).

Habitat: lodgepole pine and red fir forests, often with manzanita.

Nesting: burrows.

SIMILAR SPECIES:
Uinta Chipmunk (p. 54) has a gray crown. Yellow-pine Chipmunk (p. 20) has clear black side stripes. Least (p. 18), Alpine (p. 16) and Panamint (p. 52) chipmunks are smaller. Townsend's Chipmunk (p. 22) is larger.

Uinta Chipmunk

facial stripes are muted

eye stripe is darker immediately in front of and behind eye

stripes are distinct, with low contrast

outermost dark stripes may be nonexistant

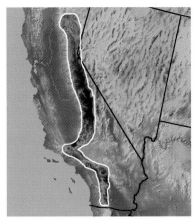

Panamint Chipmunk

Tamias panamintinus

This richly colored chipmunk has distinctive facial stripes—where other chipmunks have either two brown or two black stripes on each side of the face, this chipmunk has a black stripe above each eye and a brown stripe below each eye. The outermost dark stripes on the Panamint Chipmunk's back are indistinct or nonexistent. Similar in habits to the Cliff Chipmunk (p. 36), the Panamint Chipmunk likewise thrives among boulders and on rocky outcroppings or cliffs, but generally to the west of the Cliff Chipmunk's range—this species is named for the Panamint Mountains of southern Nevada and California, which fall in the center of its range.

ID: brightly colored, reddish appearance; outermost dark stripes are indistinct; head is gray on top; ears are tawny.

Size: *L* 7 1/2–8 5/8 in (19–22 cm); *Wt* 1 1/2–2 1/4 oz (43–64 g).

Habitat: rocky areas of piñon pine and juniper forests.

Nesting: burrows; less frequently leafy tree nests.

On occasion, Panamint Chipmunks climb trees in search of seeds and cones. Some individuals may even build spherical nests in trees, but most prefer to nest in burrows or rock crevices. Panamint Chipmunks can be seen outside their burrows almost year-round if the weather is mild. During periods of inclement weather, these chipmunks enter a state of dormancy in their burrows, but this hibernation state rarely lasts for more than a week at a time.

Like other squirrels, Panamint Chipmunks begin their courtship and mating as soon as they emerge from their winter dens. They have an unusually long gestation of about 36 days, after which three to seven babies are born. The babies have extraordinary growth rates, which puts considerable stress on the mother. An attentive parent, she ensures they are well-fed and nurtured. Over the span of about three weeks after the young are weaned, the mother plays games with them and lets them follow her as she finds and gathers food. The sibling bonds between the youngsters are strong, and they will often stay together for several weeks after their mother has left.

SIMILAR SPECIES:
Yellow-pine Chipmunk (p. 20) has more distinct coloration. Long-eared Chipmunk (p. 48) is larger and has less distinct stripes. Lodgepole Chipmunk (p. 50) and Uinta Chipmunk (p. 54) have bicolored ears (blackish in front, whitish behind), and Uinta and Palmer's Chipmunk (p. 56) have distinct dorsal stripes.

Yellow-pine Chipmunk

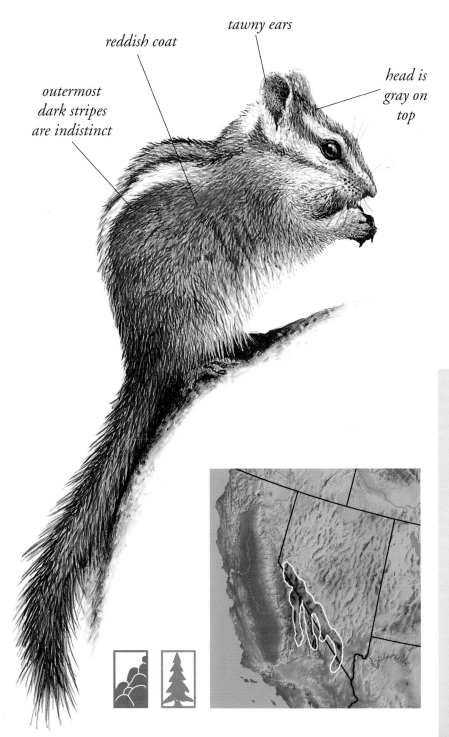

tawny ears

reddish coat

outermost
dark stripes
are indistinct

head is
gray on
top

Uinta Chipmunk

Tamias umbrinus

On the whole, chipmunk species look and behave very similarly, but the Uinta Chipmunk is one of the few species to stand out as different. Unlike most chipmunks, which prefer ground dwellings, the Uinta Chipmunk often builds its nest in a tree. As well, this deviant chipmunk puts on a large layer of fat to support itself through its winter hibernation, another unusual trait for a chipmunk. This unique chipmunk is named for the Uinta Mountains in the northeast corner of Utah, the heart of this species' range.

Uinta Chipmunks must be constantly alert for predators; threats can come from the sky, from the ground or even from below. Many raptors take a large toll on chipmunk populations, as do foxes, bobcats and snakes, but perhaps the most effective predators of chipmunks are weasels. Because weasels are small and streamlined, these voracious carnivores can sneak up on chipmunks from rock crevices or chase them into their burrows. Despite the relentless predation, some chipmunks have been known to live for five to seven years in the wild, an unusually long time for a small rodent.

ID: top of head, neck and back are grayish; sides and shoulders are brownish; stripes are dark and distinct; white undersides; black-tipped tail with light edge.

Size: L 7³/₄–9¹/₂ in (20–24 cm); Wt 2–3 oz (57–85 g).

Habitat: coniferous and mixed forests; brushy areas.

Nesting: tree nests.

Like other chipmunks, the Uinta Chipmunk is finicky about keeping clean. A chipmunk's daily bathing involves cleaning its coat with its hands and feet. Once the coat is done, the chipmunk licks its paws clean, too. When necessary, chipmunks take 'delousing' baths by rolling in dusty sand. Some of the ticks or mites in their fur get stuck in the dust and left behind. Sometimes a chipmunk's meticulous cleaning is not enough to prevent parasites, and many chipmunks are parasitized by botfly larvae, tapeworms, fleas or lice. Sick chipmunks fall first to predators, however, which helps keep diseases in check.

SIMILAR SPECIES:
Least Chipmunk (p. 18) is smaller and has darker undersides. Lodgepole Chipmunk (p. 50) has a brown forehead. Townsend's (p. 22), Long-eared (p. 48) and Cliff (p. 36) chipmunks have indistinct stripes.

Least Chipmunk

top of head,
neck and back
are grayish

stripes are dark
and distinct

sides and
shoulders are
brownish

tail has light edging
and black tip

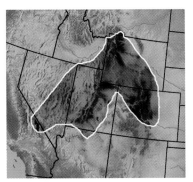

UINTA CHIPMUNK

Palmer's Chipmunk
(Charleston Mountain Chipmunk)
Tamias palmeri

The Palmer's Chipmunk has a tiny range in the mountains of Clark County, Nevada, including Charleston Mountain. The Palmer's Chipmunk's gray shoulders, well-defined stripes and preference for higher elevations distinguish it from the slightly smaller Panamint Chipmunk (p. 52), which is the only other chipmunk in its range.

The details of the Palmer's Chipmunk's life history are not known, but it probably follows a routine similar to that of other chipmunks. Before hibernation, the Palmer's Chipmunk stores large amounts of food, but it is frequently seen outside its den throughout winter. This chipmunk most likely hibernates during inclement weather, venturing out on mild winter days. This sporadic hibernation continues later into spring than that of the Panamint Chipmunk, probably because the Palmer's Chipmunk lives at higher elevations, where spring is later in arriving.

ID: dark stripes are brown to reddish; underside of tail is tawny orange; gray tinge on shoulders.

Size: *L* 8¼–8¾ in (21–22 cm); *Wt* 1¾–2½ oz (50–71 g).

Habitat: mountain coniferous forests; mahogany and manzanita regions.

Nesting: burrows.

All chipmunks, whether they hibernate or not, have an insatiable urge to store food. When a chipmunk discovers an inexhaustible supply of food, such as grain in a birdfeeder, it will carry off and stash away up to 4 qt (3.8 *l*) of food a day. To help in this task, a chipmunk's cheek pouches are well suited to carrying large numbers of seeds—when filled to capacity, they can hold at least 250 buckbrush seeds or an astonishing 1650 wild cranberry seeds.

Although chipmunks primarily save food for winter, their well-stocked larders have other uses. Because chipmunks are intolerant of extreme weather conditions, they stay inside their dens to wait out periods of very hot summer weather, happily eating from their food stores. Even a day of rain is enough to keep most chipmunks inside. A high volume of stored food provides excellent security for chipmunks, allowing them to survive periods of drought, bad weather or winter.

SIMILAR SPECIES:
Panamint Chipmunk (p. 52), the only other chipmunk in the same range, is smaller and has less contrasting stripes.

Panamint Chipmunk

gray tinge on shoulders

dark stripes are brown to reddish

underside of tail is tawny orange

Marmots

Marmots are the largest members of the squirrel family—the Hoary Marmot can reach a length of 32 in (81 cm) and a weight of 20 lb (9.1 kg). The Hoary Marmot and the Woodchuck are the best-known members of this genus, but they are only two of the six species that can be found in Canada and the United States. Marmots live in a variety of habitats, ranging from Alaska's Arctic tundra to eastern woodlands.

Sociability varies greatly among marmots: Woodchucks are the most solitary; Hoary Marmots, with their large colonies, are the most gregarious. Instead of caching large quantities of food like other squirrels, marmots prepare for winter by putting on a thick layer of fat—they will remain in a dormant state deep inside their dens throughout winter. Marmot burrows are not complex; they are usually just simple tunnels ending in a den chamber. Burrow openings, which are marked with a mound of dirt, are usually 8–12 in (20–30 cm) in diameter, but some of the larger marmots may have entrances up to 16 in (41 cm) across. Another sign of marmots in an area is their tracks, which rarely show the fifth toe on the foreprint.

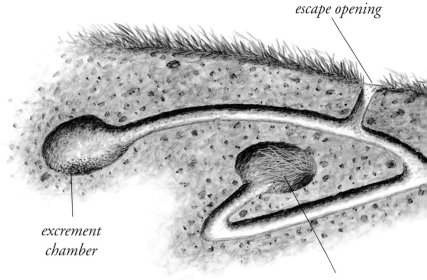

escape opening

excrement chamber

grass nest

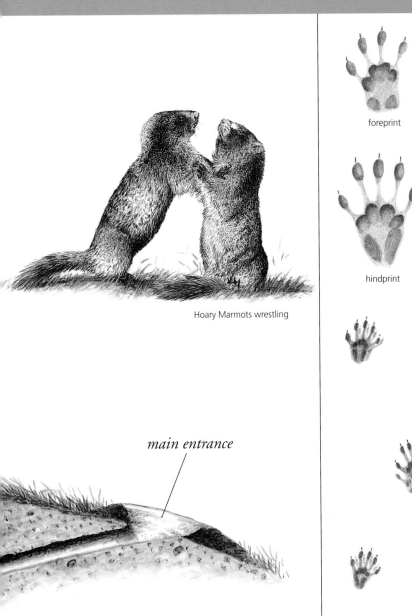

Hoary Marmots wrestling

foreprint

hindprint

main entrance

walking trail

Alaska Marmot

Marmota broweri

Of all the marmots, the Alaska Marmot is the one that biologists have studied the least. This species owes its obscurity to the remote Alaskan habitat in which it lives. In fact, so little is known about this marmot that it only recently gained status as a unique species separate from the Hoary Marmot (p. 66). The Alaska Marmot's tricolored body—a gray front, a black middle and reddish hindquarters—its frosty feet and its black-tipped guard hairs distinguish it from the Hoary Marmot. The Alaska Marmot is closely related to the Kamchatkan Marmot (*M. camtschatica*), which is also believed to have originated from the Hoary Marmot, but which probably migrated to Siberia across the Bering Strait land bridge during the Pleistocene epoch.

Alaska Marmots have short legs and long bodies, resulting in a waddling gait. They are surprisingly flexible and stretchy, however, and they can quickly hide in small spaces under rocks to evade predators, such as wolves and eagles. Marmots are such fluid and agile climbers that they resemble pearls of mercury rolling over the rocky terrain and disappearing into the cracks.

ID: 3-toned body (gray front, black middle, reddish hindquarters); black cap; grizzled gray feet; black-tipped guard hairs.

Size: *L* 22–25 in (56–64 cm); *Wt* 8–18 lb (3.6–8.2 kg).

Habitat: talus slopes; rocky areas above treeline.

Nesting: burrows.

Like most other marmots, the Alaska Marmot lives in highly sociable colonies. Especially in early spring, marmots can be seen wrestling, 'kissing,' grappling and hugging as though they missed each other's company throughout their eight months of hibernation. Marmot colonies typically contain 8 to 12 individuals: one dominant male, two females, one litter of yearlings and the current year's litter. The litter, generally about four pups, is born just two weeks after the adults emerge in spring. Gestation is about one month, however, indicating that Alaska Marmots may mate while still inside their winter burrow.

The Alaska Marmot's far northern home has a very short growing season, but this marmot manages to find enough roots, flowers, small herbaceous plants and berries to eat to fatten itself in preparation for hibernation.

SIMILAR SPECIES:
Vancouver Marmot (p. 70), the only other marmot with black-tipped guard hairs, is restricted to Vancouver Island.

Vancouver Marmot

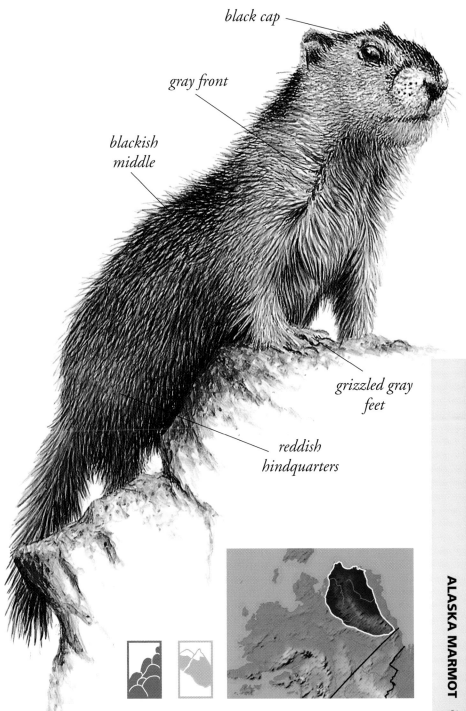

black cap

gray front

blackish
middle

grizzled gray
feet

reddish
hindquarters

Woodchuck
(Groundhog)
Marmota monax

The common Woodchuck is the subject of many tales and misconceptions. For a start, both its names are a bit misleading: the Woodchuck is not a hog, nor does it chuck wood. The name 'woodchuck' is likely derived from the Algonquian name for this animal, *wejack*. The other common name, 'groundhog,' comes from this animal's appearance in late summer—very fat and waddling low to the ground. Approximately the same size as a Yellow-bellied Marmot (p. 64), the Woodchuck has a brown head, a brown to rufous body, a blunt nose and a flattened tail. It differs most notably from other marmots in its preference for a solitary lifestyle.

Historically, the Woodchuck lived in forested areas. This marmot can still be found in woodland regions, but it now lives in great numbers on cultivated land—the Woodchuck is one of few mammal species to have prospered from human activity. Unhesitant about pilfering, Woodchucks living near humans often graze in sweet alfalfa crops to help fatten their waistlines. The luckiest Woodchucks find their way into people's backyards, where they stuff themselves on tasty apples, carrots, strawberries and other garden delights. In wild areas, Woodchucks follow the standard marmot diet of grass, leaves, seeds and berries.

Woodchucks are superb diggers that are responsible for turning over massive amounts of earth each year. Their burrows even provide lodging for other animals, such as raccoons, rabbits, salamanders and snakes. When burrowing, Woodchucks use their powerful front claws to dig and their sturdy back legs to push the dirt behind them. As they dig, they will periodically turn themselves around and bulldoze the dirt out of the tunnel using their suitably stubby heads.

ID: small to mid-sized marmot; mainly brown, with reddish to black highlights; bushy, brown tail; small ears.

Size: *L* 18–27 in (46–69 cm); *Wt* 4–12 lb (1.8–5.4 kg).

Habitat: woodlands; open fields.

Nesting: burrows.

SIMILAR SPECIES:
Yellow-bellied Marmot (p. 64) is similarly sized but has distinctly yellow undersides. Hoary Marmot (p. 66) shares much of the same range but is larger and has black feet and a frosted appearance.

Yellow-bellied Marmot

mainly brown, with reddish or black highlights

small ears

bushy, brown tail is somewhat flattened

WOODCHUCK

Yellow-bellied Marmot
(Yellow-footed Marmot, Rockchuck)

Marmota flaviventris

Colonies of Yellow-bellied Marmots have a strict social order, and banishment by the dominant male is the punishment for insubordination. Despite the rules, however, Yellow-bellied Marmots sleep late, eat heartily and snooze dreamily on warm rocks in the sun.

Whenever members of a Yellow-bellied Marmot colony are eating or wrestling with their family members, at least one marmot plays watchdog. This sentinel is responsible for warning the others if danger approaches. The alarm call is a loud chirp, which may vary in duration and intensity depending on the nature of the threat: short, steady notes probably translate as 'Everyone pay attention, something's wrong'; loud, shrill notes convey the message 'Into your burrows—Now!' Such urgent warnings are reserved for immediate dangers, such as a circling eagle or an approaching fox.

Counting hibernation and nighttime sleep, Yellow-bellied Marmots spend about 80 percent of their lives in their burrows. They like their dens to be kept clean, and when they emerge from hibernation they throw out their used bedding and replace it with fresh grass and leaves. Throughout summer, they continue to keep their bedding clean and their burrows free of debris.

While it is approximately the same size as a Woodchuck (p. 62), the Yellow-bellied Marmot's unmistakable yellow undersides make it easy to identify. It also sports a golden to rufous coat, a brown head, a yellow patch on either side of its neck and a yellow belly.

ID: tawny-brown body; distinct, yellow undersides and highlights; pale spot between eyes; bushy tail; tawny feet.

Size: *L* 19–28 in (48–71 cm); *Wt* 5–10 lb (2.3–4.5 kg).

Habitat: rocky areas; valleys; rolling hills.

Nesting: burrows.

SIMILAR SPECIES:
Woodchuck (p. 62) is darker and solidly colored. Hoary Marmot (p. 66) has black feet and its coat appears frosted.

Woodchuck

pale spots between eyes

bushy tail

yellow undersides

tawny feet

Hoary Marmot
(Rockchuck, Mountain Marmot, Whistler)
Marmota caligata

The Hoary Marmot is a common resident of the northern mountains. It is at home in rocky slopes at and above treeline, requiring only that alpine meadows are within easy reach. The champion of whistlers, its call is a piercing, shrill note that can travel for over 1 mi (1.6 km). As its name implies, the Hoary Marmot has a frosty appearance, which is due to the white-tipped guard hairs that lay overtop its gray-and-brown fur. Other distinguishing features of this marmot include black streaks on either side of the head, a reddish tail, black feet and its large size—the Hoary Marmot is the largest member of the squirrel family.

ID: large marmot; frosty appearance; brown on rump and tail; black and white markings on face; black band on nose; black feet.

Size: *L* 18–32 in (46–81 cm); *Wt* 8–20 lb (3.6–9.1 kg).

Habitat: rocky alpine slopes; alpine meadows; cliffs.

Nesting: burrows; rock crevices.

Hoary Marmots are well-known for their companionable natures and large family groups. Colonies can be so large that they are more accurately called 'villages.' A village typically has several males, many females, an assortment of yearlings and at least one litter of pups. Living in such large family groups provides good protection for each individual, because at least one marmot is always on the lookout for predators.

Daily life for Hoary Marmots involves eating two meals, dodging predators, sunbathing, hugging, nuzzling and wrestling. Their mock boxing matches frequently end in the two competitors tumbling and rolling playfully down a slope. This marmot's burrows are well-designed and are located on a slope to maximize drainage. The marmots usually excavate their sleeping chambers underneath a subsurface boulder, which protects unsuspecting squirrels from being dug up by a hungry Grizzly Bear.

SIMILAR SPECIES:
Olympic Marmot (p. 68) has more brown tones, especially on the head. Yellow-bellied Marmot (p. 64) has yellow highlights. Woodchuck (p. 62) is smaller and does not appear frosty.

Olympic Marmot

black and white
markings on face

frosty
appearance

black feet

brown rump
and tail

Olympic Marmot

Marmota olympus

Large and grizzled, the Olympic Marmot bears a close resemblance to the Hoary Marmot (p. 66). A pale band of fur over the bridge of the nose, light patches in front of the eyes and indistinct color patterns on the head separate this species from the Hoary Marmot. The best way to distinguish between these marmots, however, is by locality: Olympic Marmots are found only in subalpine regions of the Olympic Mountains in Washington, where Hoary Marmots do not occur.

ID: bushy tail; brown to golden coat; small ears; brown feet.

Size: *L* 18–31 in (46–79 cm); *Wt* 8–18 lb (3.6–8.2 kg).

Habitat: subalpine meadows and talus slopes.

Nesting: burrows.

The Olympic Marmot sleeps for several hours past sunrise. When it emerges from its burrow in the morning, it spends nearly half an hour gazing at its subalpine home. After the marmot has surveyed the land sufficiently, it waddles to a nearby meadow for breakfast. Olympic Marmots feed mainly on hardy subalpine plants, such as heathers, sedges, lilies, grasses and mosses. After a large breakfast, the marmot quickly returns to the vicinity of its burrow to spend sunny afternoons lounging and sunbathing.

For the safety of all members of a colony, at least one marmot stays alert and watches out for potential threats. If this sentinel sounds the alarm whistle, the marmots scamper to their burrow openings. Before disappearing, the marmots may pause to identify the predator: if an eagle is overhead, the marmots do not need to remain hidden for long, because the raptor will search elsewhere for an easier meal; more cunning predators, such as foxes or Mountain Lions, may wait for the marmots to resurface.

SIMILAR SPECIES:
No other marmot is regularly found on the Olympic Peninsula. Woodchuck (p. 62) has a grizzled, darker appearance and dark feet. Yellow-bellied Marmot (p. 64) has distinct golden undersides and light feet. Hoary Marmot (p. 66) has black and light facial markings and a frosty appearance.

Woodchuck

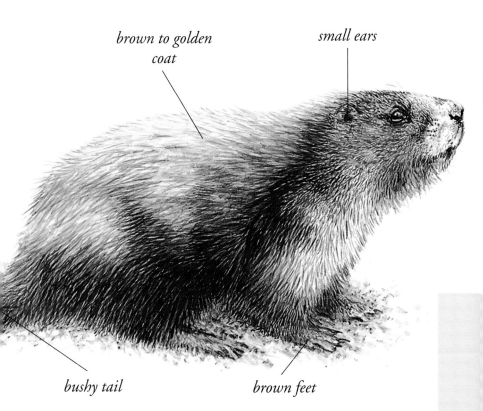

brown to golden coat

small ears

bushy tail

brown feet

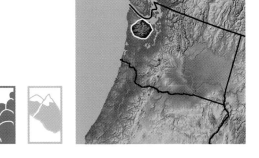

Vancouver Marmot

Marmota vancouverensis

The rarest marmot of all, the Vancouver Marmot, wears a lustrous brown coat. Perhaps numbering only several hundred, this marmot is found only in the highlands of Vancouver Island. Its unique solid-colored coat may change through the summer from deep ebony to light walnut, depending on how intensely an individual sunbathes. The annual molt for this marmot, completed in July, renews the intense dark brown of its coat.

ID: large marmot; solid, dark brown coat, fading to walnut through summer; white or buff nose; bushy tail; may have white patches on undersides.

Size: *L* 26–28 in (66–71 cm); *Wt* 6¹/₂–14 lb (2.9–6.4 kg).

Habitat: subalpine woodlands and rocky areas.

Nesting: burrows in rock crevices.

Voracious eaters, Vancouver Marmots will double or even triple in weight from May to September, gorging themselves on the lush and abundant summer food. Marmots do not store food in their burrows, so they must put on a layer of fat in the summer to last them through their cold winter hibernation.

Colonies of these shy marmots have well-structured hierarchies. A male dominates the colony and usually has a couple of females subordinate to him. Vancouver Marmots are highly sociable, and they enjoy play-fighting and nuzzling to strengthen familial bonds. The strength of these ties may be the reason that young Vancouver Marmots don't leave the colony until as late as their third year, rather than the second year, as is usual for other marmot species.

The territory of a colony is well-defined. Using scent glands on their cheeks, Vancouver Marmots mark large rocks at the limits of their home range. Antagonistic behavior is rare between marmots, but trespassers receive some intense growls and hisses. Despite the colony's patriarchy, females prove to be the more aggressive sex. Vancouver Marmots can be fearsome fighters, and both males and females are able to vigorously defend themselves when faced with predators—they have even been known to defeat their arch enemy, the Red Fox.

SIMILAR SPECIES:
Alaska Marmot (p. 60) also has black-tipped hairs, but it occurs only in northern Alaska. All other marmots have multi-colored coats and do not occur on Vancouver Island.

Alaska Marmot

white nose

white patches
on undersides

solid, dark
brown coat

bushy tail

Antelope Squirrels

The scientific name for antelope squirrels, *Ammospermophilus*, translates literally from the Greek to mean 'lover of sand and seeds,' which aptly describes the lifestyle of these striped ground squirrels. Antelope squirrels inhabit some of the hottest and driest regions of North America, and they have specific adaptations for surviving harsh desert environments. Unlike most other burrowing mammals of the desert, but like other desert squirrels, antelope squirrels are active during the day. To survive periods of extreme heat, an antelope squirrel will press its belly to the dirt in a shaded area or in its burrow to quickly draw heat out from its fur.

Unusually cold weather may confine an antelope squirrel to its burrow, but only the most northerly antelope squirrels actually hibernate for a short time—most antelope squirrels may become inactive during cold weather, but they remain awake, living off their stores of food. Antelope squirrels generally feed on seeds, green vegetation, nuts, berries, stems, roots and insects.

When these lively squirrels are fleeing from danger, they raise their tails and leap away with remarkable speed. This behavior exposes the white undersides of the tail and is reminiscent of the Pronghorn Antelope, for which these squirrels are named. Antelope squirrels are fast runners that quickly regain their burrows. Just before diving in, however, they stop for a second to chatter, chirp and stomp their feet in warning.

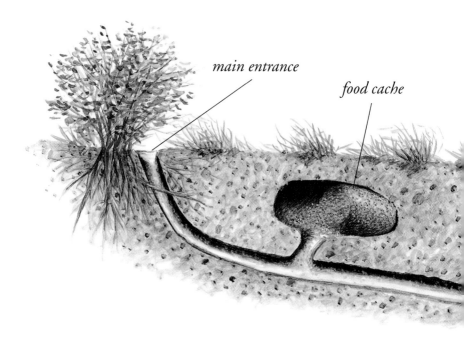

main entrance

food cache

foreprint

hindprint

running trail

White-tailed Antelope Squirrel cooling off in a bush

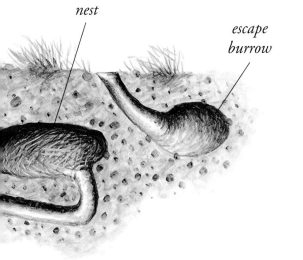

nest

escape burrow

Harris's Antelope Squirrel
(Yuma Antelope Squirrel)
Ammospermophilus harrisii

The Harris's Antelope Squirrel lives mainly in desert habitats, especially in the Yuma region of southwestern Arizona, and, more so than any other squirrel, it is able to tolerate high desert temperatures. Active at even the hottest times of the day, it scampers uninjured over cactus spines as it seeks out the tasty cactus fruit. It also dines on mesquite beans, yucca fruits and seeds, green vegetation and insects.

The Harris's Antelope Squirrel is a solitary animal, and it must be constantly alert to the presence of Coyotes, American Badgers, hawks and snakes. This squirrel makes its burrow in the sandy earth beneath desert shrubs, and, for added safety, the burrow has more than one entrance. If an antelope squirrel is deterred from its routine by a predator, it will stop just before diving into its burrow to chatter, chirp and stomp its feet.

Sometimes mistaken for a chipmunk, the Harris's Antelope Squirrel has just one pale stripe running down each side of its back. The stripe starts at the shoulder and ends at the hip, and it is not bordered on either side by a dark stripe, as is the stripe on the Golden-mantled Ground Squirrel (p. 118). The Harris's Antelope Squirrel has mainly gray fur, with tawny highlights, and it is the only antelope squirrel that does not have white on the underside of the tail.

ID: mostly gray; pink and tawny highlights; 1 white stripe down each side; gray tail.

Size: L 8⅝–10 in (22–25 cm); Wt 4–5¼ oz (110–150 g).

Habitat: deserts; scrubby flatlands.

Nesting: burrows.

SIMILAR SPECIES:
All other antelope squirrels have two-toned tails. Chipmunks (pp. 12–57) have striped faces. Golden-mantled Ground Squirrel (p. 118) is larger and has two dark stripes on either side of the pale side stripe.

White-tailed Antelope Squirrel

pink or tawny
highlights

single white
stripe down
each side

tail is gray, with no
white underneath

HARRIS'S ANTELOPE SQUIRREL

White-tailed Antelope Squirrel

Ammospermophilus leucurus

The most widespread of any *Ammospermophilus* species, the White-tailed Antelope Squirrel is comfortable in a variety of different habitats: deserts, valley bottoms, gravelly washes, sagebrush plateaus and foothills all make suitable homes for this ground dweller. In the northern parts of its range, the White-tailed Antelope Squirrel may hibernate for about two months. As a whole, however, antelope squirrels are non-hibernating—their special adaptations are for surviving hot desert environments, rather than cold winter conditions. When extreme desert heat causes them discomfort, antelope squirrels may press their bellies to the dirt in shaded areas or climb into shady shrubs to maximize the air circulation around them.

White-tailed Antelope Squirrels live in large aggregations, with each adult maintaining at least one burrow. An adult's home burrow is its longest and best maintained burrow; any auxiliary or escape burrows are short. A strict social order is established among the males living together: the young males challenge each other to boxing matches, with the winner gaining a superior position in the hierarchy.

Often mistaken for a chipmunk, this antelope squirrel has a distinct pale band down each side. In summer, the White-tailed Antelope Squirrel has a tawny coat; in winter its coat is cast with gray. As its name suggests, the underside of the tail is stark white.

ID: mainly tawny in summer; grayish in winter; 1 white stripe down each side; pale undersides; 1 dark stripe running down tail; underside of tail is white.

Size: L 7⅝–9⅜ in (19–24 cm); Wt 3–5½ oz (85–156 g).

Habitat: deserts; foothills; sage and creosote flats.

Nesting: burrows.

SIMILAR SPECIES:
Nelson's Antelope Squirrel (p. 80) is more tawny overall.

Nelson's Antelope Squirrel

single pale stripe
down each side

dark stripe
runs the length
of the tail

pale
undersides

tail is white
underneath

mainly tawny colored
in summer

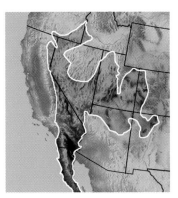

77

Texas Antelope Squirrel

Ammospermophilus interpres

Most of the antelope squirrels have tawny or cinnamon highlights, but the Texas Antelope Squirrel is uniformly dark gray. It has one white band down each side and two distinct black stripes on the upper surface of its white-bottomed tail.

Like many squirrels, antelope squirrels have a tendency to sleep late. Texas Antelope Squirrels do not emerge from their burrows until after 8:00 a.m., when the desert has warmed up to their liking. Their preferred habitat is the rough, rocky terrain associated with deserts: canyon walls, gravelly washes and rough scrubby areas are well-suited to their needs. Texas Antelope Squirrels like the protection afforded by sparse rocks and bushes, but dense cover prevents them from seeing approaching predators—they must be constantly alert for hawks, rattlesnakes, weasels, ravens and roadrunners.

ID: brown to grayish body; 1 white stripe down each side; underside of tail is white; may have 2 black stripes on either side of tail.

Size: *L* 8⅝–9¼ in (22–24 cm); *Wt* 3–4½ oz (85–128 g).

Habitat: rough terrain; deserts; creosote bush flats.

Nesting: burrows.

Although they do not hibernate or estivate, Texas Antelope Squirrels put on a layer of fat during summer, which affords them extra security during the winter months, when food may be hard to find. Unusually cold weather may confine them to their burrows, and food caches, which the squirrels diligently collect during summer, also sustain them through the winter. These antelope squirrels mainly eat creosote, yucca and juniper seeds, cactus pulp and fruit, mesquite beans and insects.

Although Texas Antelope Squirrels are well-equipped to dig their own burrows, they frequently use the abandoned burrows of other animals. Each burrow has more than one entrance and is about 10 ft (3 m) long. Adults often maintain auxiliary burrows as handy refuges when they are in danger.

SIMILAR SPECIES:
White-tailed Antelope Squirrel (p. 76) is very similar, but has only one black stripe on the tail.

White-tailed Antelope Squirrel

underside of tail
is white

single white
stripe down
each side

brownish or
grayish body

Nelson's Antelope Squirrel
(San Joaquin Antelope Squirrel)

Ammospermophilus nelsoni

A threatened species living only in the deserts of California, the Nelson's Antelope Squirrel is the rarest member of its genus. It is also the largest antelope squirrel. This ground dweller is a pale tawny color overall, and like the other antelope squirrels, it has a single pale stripe down each side of its body.

ID: tawny-yellow body; 1 white stripe down each side; underside of tail is white.

Size: *L* 9–11 in (23–28 cm); *Wt* 5¹/₂ oz (160 g).

Habitat: rolling desert country; sandy washes; shrubby flats.

Nesting: burrows.

Nelson's Antelope Squirrels inhabit rocky and scrubby desert areas and feed mainly on insects, seeds and cactus. They live in close association with Horned Larks and White-crowned Sparrows, which unwittingly act as sentinels for these squirrels. When Nelson's Antelope Squirrels are feeding or playing, they do not stay constantly alert for predators; instead, they listen for the larks or sparrows to give the alarm that a predator is near.

The adult antelope squirrels mate in either late winter or early spring, and the females bear one litter of 6 to 11 young a year, after about 26 days of gestation. The young are totally helpless at birth, but their growth rates are remarkable—within six weeks the youngsters are nearly indistinguishable from the adults.

Extremely hot conditions will cause Nelson's Antelope Squirrels to either retreat to their burrows or to climb into the branches of shady bushes to catch a cooling breeze. Although the desert weather can be severe and food scarce, these antelope squirrels do not hibernate or estivate. California Ground Squirrels (p. 112) often live among antelope squirrels and eat many of the same foods, but very little competition exists between these species, because the ground squirrels spend five to eight months of the year dormant in their burrows—from November to February, the scarce food sources are eaten solely by Nelson's Antelope Squirrels.

SIMILAR SPECIES:
White-tailed Antelope Squirrel (p. 76) is smaller and duller gray over the back.

White-tailed Antelope Squirrel

tawny-yellow
body

white stripe down
each side

underside of tail
is white

Ground Squirrels

The genus *Spermophilus* is the most widespread group of squirrels—ground squirrels inhabit areas ranging from the barren Arctic tundra to hot southern deserts. Ground squirrels are less gregarious than prairie-dogs, but they are nevertheless found in aggregations where food is abundant. They are strictly diurnal and spend the day feeding on grasses, seeds, roots, green vegetation, insects and sometimes carrion.

Most species of ground squirrels hibernate during winter; their heart rate, metabolism and respiration all slow, and in this state they 'sleep' through winter. Several ground squirrels also estivate during late summer. Estivation resembles hibernation, but it is used to outlast periods of extremely hot, dry summer weather. Most ground squirrels that estivate continue their dormancy right through winter until the following spring. Courtship and mating occur in spring, immediately after the ground squirrels emerge from hibernation.

Ground squirrel burrows may be simple or intricate, but they usually have a regular sleeping chamber, a winter chamber and at least two entrances, which helps the squirrels elude their many predators. Ground squirrels are champion whistlers, with a variety of calls to mean 'danger' or 'the coast is clear' or simply for familial smalltalk. Despite their many precautions, ground squirrels regularly fall prey to snakes, hawks, eagles, weasels, foxes, Coyotes and other carnivores. The life expectancy of these ground dwellers is less than four years. Individuals that manage to elude predators may live for as long as six years.

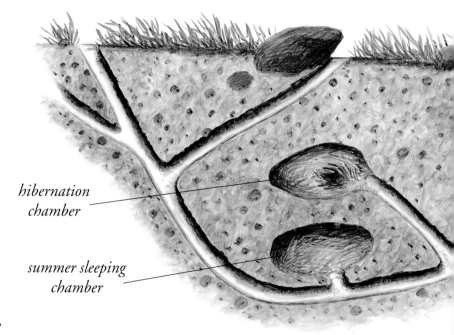

hibernation chamber

summer sleeping chamber

Golden-mantled Ground Squirrel with full cheek pouches

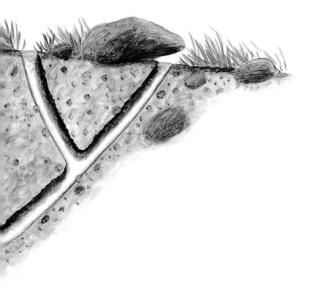

foreprint

hindprint

running trail

Arctic Ground Squirrel
(Parka Squirrel)
Spermophilus parryii

Not surprisingly, the Arctic Ground Squirrel is the only member of its genus living in the northern tundra, where the climate is harsh and food can be scarce. In this sparse habitat, the Arctic Ground Squirrel eats green vegetation, roots, fungi and the inner bark of many woody plants. It hibernates for more than six months of the year to avoid the long winters of cold and darkness. To prepare for hibernation, this squirrel must put on a layer of fat and store some non-perishable foods in its winter den. The fat will sustain it through winter, and the stored food is a ready meal for when it awakes in spring.

ID: large ground squirrel; reddish-brown to gray body with some white dappling in coat; reddish head and shoulders; yellow to tawny undersides.

Size: *L* 12–16 in (30–39 cm); *Wt* 25–28 oz (710–790 g).

Habitat: tundra; subalpine brushy areas.

Nesting: shallow burrows.

In the summer months, Arctic Ground Squirrels experience many weeks of constant sunlight. Despite the lack of night, however, they maintain a regular routine: they rise each 'morning' at about 4:00 a.m. and retire to their burrows at about 9:00 p.m.

A major challenge facing these ground dwellers is permafrost—in most parts of their range the ground is permanently frozen. Permafrost areas, which are ill-suited to burrowing, are used by these squirrels as feeding grounds; it is only in local areas of little or no permafrost that they can burrow. Ideal habitats for burrows include sandy banks, lake-shores and meadows with good drainage. The burrows usually descend no more than 3 ft (91 cm) below the surface. When large colonies form, the intertwined burrows may amount to more than 70 ft (21 m) of tunnels.

SIMILAR SPECIES:
Columbian Ground Squirrel (p. 86) is also large and richly colored, but it is redder overall, it has less distinct dappling, and the two species' ranges overlap only in northeastern British Columbia.

Columbian Ground Squirrel

head and shoulders
are reddish

reddish-brown to
gray body with
white dapples

yellow to tawny
undersides

Columbian Ground Squirrel

Spermophilus columbianus

Large and richly colored, the Columbian Ground Squirrel is distinguished from the other ground squirrels by its red face. It is among the largest of the ground squirrels, reaching at least 17 in (43 cm) in length, and by mid- to late summer it is also the heaviest ground squirrel, weighing up to 29 oz (820 g).

The Columbian Ground Squirrel spends about two-thirds of the year in its burrow: the winter months are spent in hibernation, immediately preceded by a late-summer estivation. Before entering estivation, a Columbian Ground Squirrel must put on a thick layer of fat if it is to survive the coming eight months without food. Adults must increase their weight by about 60 percent before going into their dens. Immature ground squirrels born earlier in the year are the last to enter their dens—they must eat enough to increase their weight (from birth) by 3000 percent before they are ready for dormancy. The Columbian Ground Squirrel's diet includes green vegetation, seeds, roots, insects and even small vertebrates.

ID: grayish to tawny body; reddish-brown face, forelegs, feet and belly; bushy, reddish tail is edged with white.

Size: *L* 13–16 in (33–41 cm); *Wt* 12–29 oz (340–820 g).

Habitat: alpine meadows; brushy areas; grasslands.

Nesting: burrows.

Columbian Ground Squirrels live in small colonies. In spring, the courtship battles between males include side-to-side shoving, head-on collisions and ramming each other in the hindquarters. These battles might be mistaken for playful 'bumper car' games if not for the deep, bleeding wounds that are often inflicted. Females bear three to seven young, which grow quickly during spring and early summer.

SIMILAR SPECIES:
Arctic Ground Squirrel (p. 84), which enters the Columbian's range in northeastern British Columbia, has distinct white dappling through its coat. Most other ground squirrels in the same range are much smaller, and none has the same combination of a reddish face, forelegs and feet.

Arctic Ground Squirrel

grayish to tawny-brown body

reddish-brown face

reddish forelegs, feet and belly

bushy, reddish tail is edged with white

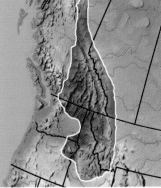

Townsend's Ground Squirrel

Spermophilus townsendii

The Townsend's Ground Squirrel is one of the ground squirrels that has earned the nickname 'gopher'—the French Canadian word *gaufre* means 'honeycomb,' a perfect description of a large colony's maze of underground tunnels. This species has an unmottled coat that is usually smoke gray in color, with tawny or even pinkish highlights. There is sometimes, but not always, a light cinnamon color on the underside of the tail, on the cheeks and around the hindlegs.

Townsend's Ground Squirrels are colonial, yet somewhat antisocial, ground dwellers: although they live in colonies that can be very large, friendly behavior is reserved for immediate family members only. Like other ground squirrels, Townsend's Ground Squirrels utter shrill squeaks to keep colony members in contact and multi-note trills to warn of danger. American Badgers, foxes, hawks and Coyotes are the main predators for which they must be constantly alert.

ID: small, gray squirrel with pink highlights; pale undersides; short tail is fringed with white and reddish underneath.

Size: L 6⁵/₈–11 in (17–28 cm); Wt 4¹/₂–12 oz (130–340 g).

Habitat: arid flatlands; deserts; sagebrush regions; rarely in humid lowlands.

Nesting: burrows.

Eating an omnivorous diet, the Townsend's Ground Squirrel dines on seeds, green vegetation, insects and carrion. It both estivates and hibernates, starting in July and lasting at least until the end of January. Before July, a squirrel requires 120 to 135 days of heavy eating to sufficiently fatten itself for dormancy. Females and juveniles usually take a bit longer to do this than males. If an individual has not put on enough weight to survive until February, it may wake during fall to feed again after only a short period of estivation. Ideally, the squirrels remain dormant for the entire seven months. In some of the warmer parts of its range, the Townsend's Ground Squirrel may not hibernate at all.

Recently, some biologists have separated the Townsend's Ground Squirrel into three species. Under this classification, the name 'Townsend's Ground Squirrel' is reserved for the populations in south-central Washington; the other two species are the Columbia Plateau Ground Squirrel (*S. canus*) and the Great Basin Ground Squirrel (*S. mollis*).

SIMILAR SPECIES:
Most other ground squirrels occurring in the same range are larger. Washington Ground Squirrel (p. 90) has a dappled coat and a black-tipped tail.

Washington Ground Squirrel

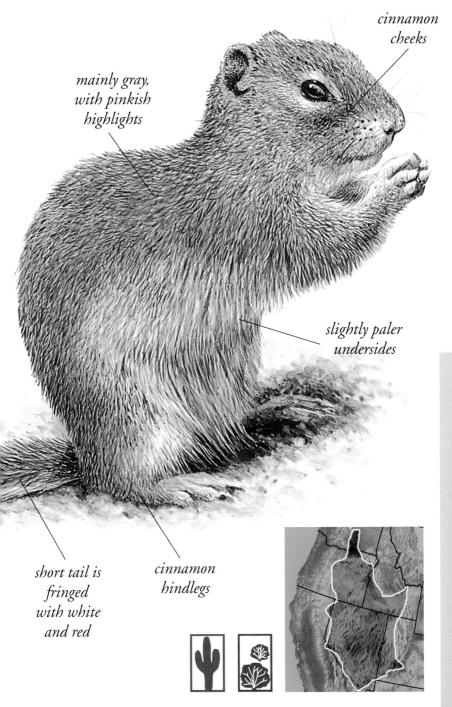

cinnamon cheeks

mainly gray, with pinkish highlights

slightly paler undersides

short tail is fringed with white and red

cinnamon hindlegs

Washington Ground Squirrel

Spermophilus washingtoni

The Washington Ground Squirrel is a medium-sized, gray squirrel with indistinct white flecks throughout its coat. The features that help distinguish it from the other species of ground squirrels are its cinnamon-tinted nose, its reddish hindlegs and its short, black-tipped tail. It lives primarily in grasslands with scattered sagebrush; it avoids densely covered areas where it cannot see the land around its burrow.

Washington Ground Squirrels spend about seven months of the year dormant. Starting in July, or even as early as June, they enter estivation earlier than most ground squirrels. Often, late summer is too hot and food is too scarce for the ground squirrels to survive; instead, they put on a large layer of fat by eating heavily from March until July, and then become dormant until late February. Washington Ground Squirrels fatten themselves on green vegetation, seedling crops, seeds, flowers and some insects.

ID: mainly gray squirrel with light dapples throughout coat; pale undersides; reddish highlights on hindlegs and nose; short, black-tipped tail.

Size: *L* 7¼–9⅝ in (18–24 cm); *Wt* 5⅜–10 oz (150–280 g).

Habitat: meadows and grasslands; open brushy areas.

Nesting: burrows.

In mid-February, after emerging from hibernation, the adults mate. Males often battle for females, because the females are only receptive for a short while. In mid-March, a litter of about eight young is born. The tiny squirrels are helpless and blind and urgently require their mother's milk. The mother feeds them for about four weeks, until they are a little more than half grown and ready to be weaned. By the eighth week, the young are almost indistinguishable from the adults. Such rapid growth rates are necessary for the youngsters, which must reach near-adult size and put on a layer of fat for hibernation in only about 100 days.

SIMILAR SPECIES:
Townsend's Ground Squirrel (p. 88) and Belding's Ground Squirrel (p. 100) have undappled coats. Columbian Ground Squirrel (p. 86) is much larger and has much more red throughout its coat.

Townsend's Ground Squirrel

mainly gray, with
light dapples

reddish
nose

reddish hindlegs

black-tipped
tail

Idaho Ground Squirrel

Spermophilus brunneus

The Idaho Ground Squirrel, the rarest *Spermophilus* species in North America, lives in only a few valleys of western Idaho. It sports a white chin, golden highlights and a red nose, and its coat is dappled gray over most of the back. This ground squirrel's tail is beautiful, with five to eight alternating, dark and light bands.

Awake for only one-third of the year, Idaho Ground Squirrels begin their dormancy with a late-summer estivation, during which time they have a greatly slowed metabolism, heart rate and respiration, as in winter hibernation. Idaho Ground Squirrels enter their burrows in late July or August, when the weather is often too hot and dry for their liking, and their dormancy continues until the following spring, nearly eight months later.

ID: mottled grayish brown over back; light yellowish-gray belly, shoulders and underside of tail; white chin; rusty-red nose; brownish rump; tawny to golden forelegs; rufous hindlegs; tail is banded with alternating dark and light brown tones.

Size: *L* 8¹/₄–8⁵/₈ in (21–22 cm); *Wt* 3¹/₂–4⁵/₈ oz (99–131 g).

Habitat: arid, open areas with little vegetation.

Nesting: burrows.

The burrows excavated by these colonial ground squirrels are long and complex. The winter burrows, which are added as extensions to the summer burrows, are blocked off with plugs of grass or earth, both in summer, to protect the hibernation chamber, and in winter, when the squirrels are dormant. These squirrels may have a cache of food handy inside the winter chamber to give themselves a guaranteed meal when they emerge in spring.

When the ground squirrels emerge from hibernation, they immediately begin looking for food and mates—they only have four months, from late March to late July, to mate, raise their young and fatten their girths. The year's youngsters don't emerge from their dens until mid-May, so they face the formidable task of eating enough food to reach adult size and put on a layer of fat in about three months. To prepare for their long dormancy, Idaho Ground Squirrels eat green vegetation, seeds, grasses and tasty wild onions. Like other ground squirrels, they also consume some animal protein, such as insects or small vertebrates.

SIMILAR SPECIES:
Columbian Ground Squirrel (p. 86) is larger, has more red on its face and does not have a white chin.

Columbian Ground Squirrel

mottled grayish brown
over the back

reddish nose

tawny to
golden forelegs

rufous hindlegs

tail is banded with
alternating dark
and light tones

Richardson's Ground Squirrel
(Flickertail, Picket Pin)
Spermophilus richardsonii

A well-known prairie inhabitant, the Richardson's Ground Squirrel is frequently nicknamed 'flickertail,' because of the conspicuous tail flick that accompanies its shrill whistle. Another common nickname for this ground squirrel is 'gopher.' An over-used name, 'gopher' has also been given to several other species of ground squirrels, a separate group of burrowing rodents, a tortoise and a snake.

Generally tawny gray in appearance, the Richardson's Ground Squirrel has dark but indistinct dapples and bars down its back. Its undersides are pale or white, as are the edges of its tail. Usually solitary, this ground squirrel may live in groups where food is abundant. It is frequently seen sitting upright at its burrow entrance as it surveys its surroundings.

ID: tawny-gray body; paler undersides; tail is tawny above, light buff below.

Size: *L* 9³/₄–14 in (25–36 cm); *Wt* 13–17 oz (370–480 g).

Habitat: prairies.

Nesting: burrows.

Richardson's Ground Squirrels have earned quite a reputation for plundering grain crops and digging up farmland, an impressive accomplishment for creatures that spend 90 percent of their lives in a burrow. Counting nighttime, hot afternoons and eight months of hibernation, few mammals in North America live such retired lifestyles. Their long dormancy begins with estivation, usually starting in mid-August, although sometimes as early as July, to survive the hot, barren summer weather.

Upon emerging from hibernation in March, males eagerly await the late emergence of the females. Mating occurs in March, and the litter is born just less than a month later. The newborn young are tiny and helpless, and they are faced with four months of rapid growth. Beginning with their mother's milk, they increase their weight from ¹/₄ oz (7 g) to about 4³/₄ oz (130 g) in their first six weeks. To reach their adult size, they feed on seeds, vegetation, insects and carrion.

SIMILAR SPECIES:
Belding's Ground Squirrel (p. 100) has a dark dorsal stripe. Franklin's Ground Squirrel (p. 108) is larger and has darker undersides. Other ground squirrels in the same range are not as plainly colored.

Belding's Ground Squirrel

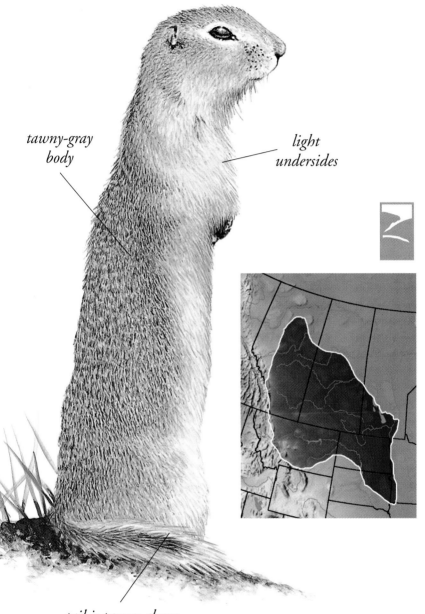

tawny-gray
body

light
undersides

tail is tawny above,
light buff below

Wyoming Ground Squirrel

Spermophilus elegans

A medium-sized squirrel, this grassland and montane inhabitant has a buffy-gray or tawny appearance. With little color variation to distinguish it from other ground dwellers, the Wyoming Ground Squirrel's best field mark is its cinnamon-colored nose. The Belding's Ground Squirrel (p. 100), which occurs in some of the same areas, has a pinkish nose.

Most of the ground squirrels that live in areas with hot, dry summers enter dormancy in early August. From that time until the following March, their environment is either too hot, too cold or too barren for their comfort. Rather than live in adverse conditions, Wyoming Ground Squirrels spend seven to eight months of the year dormant in the nest chambers of their underground burrows.

ID: tawny-gray body; paler undersides; cinnamon-colored nose; long tail is edged with light hairs.

Size: L 10–12 in (25–30 cm); Wt 7³/₈–11 oz (210–310 g).

Habitat: montane meadows; grasslands; sage flats; rocky slopes.

Nesting: burrows.

In favorable habitats, Wyoming Ground Squirrels live in groups that give the appearance of a colony, but this species is not truly colonial. Even in these group settings, the individual Wyoming Ground Squirrels build separate burrows—truly colonial ground squirrels share their burrows and follow a social hierarchy.

Most ground squirrels have a shrill, whistle-like warning call, but the Wyoming Ground Squirrel is distinguished by its cricket-like chirp. This quiet, trilling call, which is audible only to other squirrels in the immediate vicinity, is used to warn others when a predator is approaching. The Wyoming Ground Squirrel's most serious predators include American Badgers, hawks, weasels, foxes and Bobcats. In turn, this omnivorous squirrel eats a diet of seeds, green vegetation, insects and carrion.

SIMILAR SPECIES:
Townsend's Ground Squirrel (p. 88) is smaller. Belding's Ground Squirrel (p. 100) has a pink nose and pinkish highlights. Uinta Ground Squirrel (p. 98) has black flecks on the underside of the tail.

Townsend's Ground Squirrel

tawny-brown body

*cinnamon-
colored nose*

*long tail is edged
with light hairs*

Uinta Ground Squirrel

Spermophilus armatus

Distinguished only by its cinnamon-colored nose and gray cheeks, the Uinta Ground Squirrel may be hard to identify. The overall color of an adult is tawny gray, with light undersides and pale forelegs. In contrast to the body, the hindlegs are cinnamon colored, like the nose. The tawny-colored tail, which is sprinkled with black, helps to distinguish the Uinta Ground Squirrel from other tawny-colored species, such as the Richardson's Ground Squirrel (p. 94).

Where food is abundant, Uinta Ground Squirrels live in large colonies. They excavate complex burrow systems that house all the colony members. Considerable amounts of earth are overturned by these diggers, which thereby contribute to soil aeration and nutrient cycling.

Like other ground dwellers, Uinta Ground Squirrels favor mild weather. So intolerant of hot, dry weather are these squirrels that they begin estivation in summer to avoid the extreme weather conditions of late July and August. A few individuals may forego early estivation, but by September all Uinta Ground Squirrels are below ground. Their dormancy continues until late March, when the males emerge. The females don't appear until early April, after nearly nine months of dormancy.

Uinta Ground Squirrels are busy during the four months that they are awake. They mate in April, and after about 28 days of gestation, four to seven pink, helpless young are born. The infants are facing a difficult three months: they must eat ravenously in order to grow to adult length and fatten themselves sufficiently to survive their first eight months of dormancy.

ID: large ground squirrel; mainly buff-brown; lighter undersides; cinnamon-colored face and hindlegs; mainly brown tail, with black flecks and light edge.

Size: *L* 11–12 in (28–30 cm); *Wt* 10–15 oz (280–430 g).

Habitat: dry sagebrush regions; mowed areas.

Nesting: burrows.

SIMILAR SPECIES:
Belding's Ground Squirrel (p. 100) has a brown band down its back. Richardson's Ground Squirrel (p. 94) has a pale, clay-colored tail. Townsend's Ground Squirrel (p. 88) has a shorter tail with a cinnamon underside.

Belding's Ground Squirrel

mainly buff-brown coat

cinnamon-colored face

light undersides

cinnamon-colored
hindlegs

mainly brown tail,
with black flecks and
a light edge

Belding's Ground Squirrel

Spermophilus beldingi

The richly colored Belding's Ground Squirrel is easy to distinguish from other species of ground squirrels by its combination of a broad, chestnut brown stripe down its back and pinkish undersides. This ground squirrel has a slightly pinkish tone overall, and the top of its head, its chin, its forelegs and the underside of its tail are cinnamon pink.

Several ground squirrels, including the Belding's Ground Squirrel, estivate in late summer, giving them the longest dormancies of any North American mammals. The Belding's Ground Squirrel enters its estivation in August, and this summer dormancy continues on to become hibernation. This squirrel spends two-thirds of the year dormant, not waking until mid- to late March.

During the four months that Belding's Ground Squirrels are awake, they must consume large amounts of food to put on the thick layer of fat they will need to survive the following winter. These ground squirrels eat a diet of grains, green vegetation, seeds, insects and small vertebrates to at least double their weight before they re-enter dormancy.

As with all other squirrels, the males emerge from their winter burrows first. In some parts of their range, they may have to tunnel through a layer of snow blocking the burrow entrance. The females emerge from the burrow one or two weeks later, after the snow has melted. About five days after the females emerge, they are receptive to mating. The males, which have been ready since they emerged three weeks earlier, battle each other fiercely for the females. The fighting is intense because the females are receptive for only three to six hours.

ID: large, grayish-brown ground squirrel; pink highlights on face and undersides; broad brown stripe running down back; black-tipped tail.

Size: *L* 9–12 in (23–30 cm); *Wt* 8–12 oz (230–340 g).

Habitat: subalpine meadows; grassy areas, including farmlands and mowed areas.

Nesting: burrows.

Richardson's Ground Squirrel

SIMILAR SPECIES:
Richardson's Ground Squirrel (p. 94) has a distinct, clay-colored tail. Townsend's Ground Squirrel (p. 88) is smaller and lacks the pink highlights.

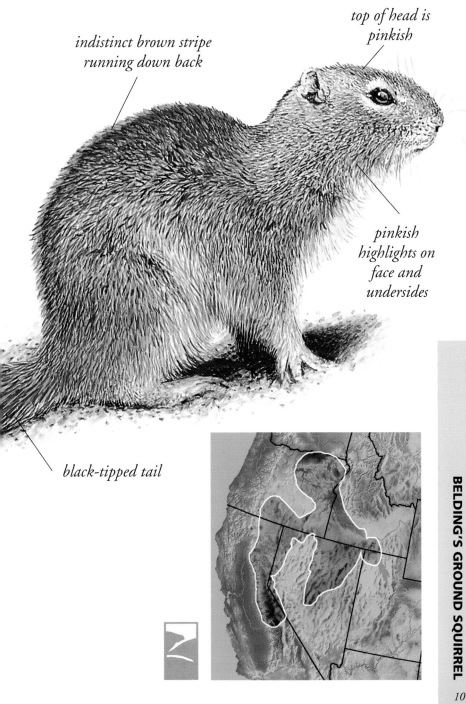

top of head is pinkish

indistinct brown stripe running down back

pinkish highlights on face and undersides

black-tipped tail

Thirteen-lined Ground Squirrel

Spermophilus tridecemlineatus

The Thirteen-lined Ground Squirrel is common only in the shortgrass prairie of central North America. Even where it is locally abundant, this squirrel is not often seen, because its striped and spotted back renders it nearly invisible in the prairie grass. Typically, this ground squirrel has 13 rows of light-colored stripes and spots down its dark brown back. A quick count of the stripes, however, often reveals fewer or more than the named 13 lines. Near the Mexican border, a Thirteen-lined Ground Squirrel with fewer than 13 stripes can be confused with a Mexican Ground Squirrel (p. 104), which has nine pale rows of blotchy spots down its back.

ID: tawny brown overall; 13 alternating solid and spotted, light-colored stripes down dark brown back; long, thin tail is fringed with white.

Size: *L* 6³/₄–12 in (17–30 cm); *Wt* 3⁷/₈–9¹/₂ oz (110–270 g).

Habitat: shortgrass prairie; fields; golf courses; shrubby areas.

Nesting: burrows.

Thirteen-lined Ground Squirrels often live in aggregations, but, during their active months, adults are antagonistic toward each other, and each squirrel digs a separate burrow. The manner in which these ground squirrels dig their burrows is rather peculiar: as a squirrel digs, it carries away the dirt in its mouth, thereby leaving no mound of dirt to give away the entrance to its burrow. At night, the squirrel will also tamp grass or dirt into the entrance to further hide its whereabouts.

Thirteen-lined Ground Squirrels have a predilection for eating grasshoppers, in addition to their regular diet of grasses and seeds, so while these ground squirrels may cause some damage to a farmer's seedling crops, they more than make up for it by eating great numbers of harmful insects. By the end of summer, these stripy beasts have consumed so much food that they are fat, irritable and ready for bed. The listless squirrels curl into tight balls in their solitary nest chambers, where they will stay for about seven months.

Mexican Ground Squirrel

SIMILAR SPECIES:
Spotted Ground Squirrel (p. 106) has unorganized spots over its grayish-brown back. Mexican Ground Squirrel (p. 104) has nine distinct rows of solid and spotted, light-colored stripes down its back.

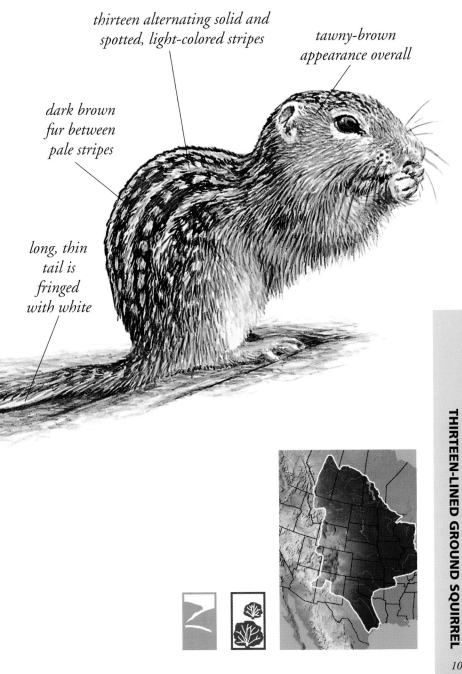

thirteen alternating solid and
spotted, light-colored stripes

tawny-brown
appearance overall

dark brown
fur between
pale stripes

long, thin
tail is
fringed
with white

Mexican Ground Squirrel

Spermophilus mexicanus

Similar in appearance to the Thirteen-lined Ground Squirrel (p. 102), the Mexican Ground Squirrel is adorned with alternating dark and light stripes and blotchy spots down its back. The Mexican Ground Squirrel can be properly identified by the number of stripes: on the rich brown base color, it has nine rows of pale, square spots, with every second row more distinctly spotted than the others.

The Mexican Ground Squirrel lives in a variety of low-elevation habitats, including shrubby grasslands and mesquite or cactus deserts. The food choices available to it in these dry regions are limited, but it seems to thrive on mesquite leaves and beans, cactus fruits and insects. This ground squirrel also has slight predaceous tendencies, and some individuals may kill and eat small vertebrates, such as young rabbits. The Mexican Ground Squirrel does not need to put on a large layer of fat in a short period of time like its cousins do—if it hibernates at all, it is intermittent and short lived.

Fine diggers, Mexican Ground Squirrels make their burrows in sandy or gravelly soil. They live in loose colonies, and each adult has several burrows, one of which is the 'active,' or 'home,' burrow. The auxiliary burrows may be older ones in poor repair, but they are kept open to serve as refuges in case of emergency. The nesting chamber, where individuals sleep and mothers raise their young, is in the deepest part of the home burrow. When these squirrels enter their burrows to sleep, they plug the entrances with grass or earth. To find the burrow of a Mexican Ground Squirrel, look near the base of a cactus, it is a favorite burrowing spot.

ID: mainly brown; about 9 rows of pale stripes, alternating spotted and nearly solid, down dark brown back; cream-colored undersides; long, bushy tail.

Size: *L* 11–15 in (28–38 cm); *Wt* 4³/₄–12 oz (130–340 g).

Habitat: brushy and grassy regions; deserts.

Nesting: burrows.

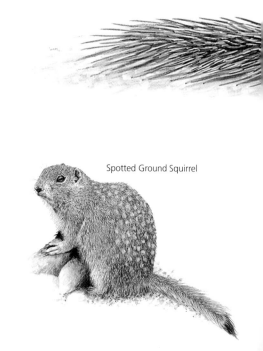

Spotted Ground Squirrel

SIMILAR SPECIES:
Spotted Ground Squirrel (p. 106) has unorganized spots all over its back. Thirteen-lined Ground Squirrel (p. 102) has about 13 rows of solid and spotty stripes.

nine rows of light stripes, alternating spotted and nearly solid

body is mainly brown

cream-colored undersides

long, fairly bushy tail

Spotted Ground Squirrel

Spermophilus spilosoma

This small squirrel earned its name from the pale, squarish spots it has over its back. The Spotted Ground Squirrel is mainly gray or tawny brown, with a pale belly, and it lives in either dry, sandy areas or sparse pine woods in Arizona and New Mexico, and from Texas to South Dakota. Two other species of ground squirrels with spots are found in some of the same areas: the Mexican Ground Squirrel (p. 104) has about nine neat rows of light-colored spots; the Thirteen-lined Ground Squirrel (p. 102) has about 13 rows of light-colored spots and stripes.

Most ground squirrels cannot tolerate extreme temperatures, and they must confine their active periods to mornings and late afternoons. Spotted Ground Squirrels are no exception: in the dry heat of their southern homes, these squirrels spend hot afternoons in their burrows. The tiny tunnels leading to their underground dens are only about 2 in (5 cm) wide, and they can be found under bushes or overhanging rocks. Spotted Ground Squirrels are mainly solitary, and each individual excavates one long tunnel that ends in a nest chamber. The main passageway is up to 12 ft (3.7 m) long, and it has a hidden second entrance that the squirrel can use to quickly evade predators.

ID: mainly grayish brown; scattered and indistinct pale spots over back; pale undersides; thin, black-tipped tail.

Size: *L* 7¹/₄–10 in (18–25 cm); *Wt* 3¹/₂–4³/₈ oz (99–124 g).

Habitat: grasslands; forest edges; sandy flats.

Nesting: burrows.

In the southern parts of their range, Spotted Ground Squirrels do not hibernate—for the entire year they feed aboveground, mainly on cactus pulp, mesquite beans, green vegetation, seeds and insects. In more northern parts, these squirrels will hibernate for short periods, usually just two or three months, and only during severe weather.

SIMILAR SPECIES:
Thirteen-lined Ground Squirrel (p. 102) has about 13 rows of spots and stripes. Mexican Ground Squirrel (p. 104) has nine rows of spots.

Thirteen-lined Ground Squirrel

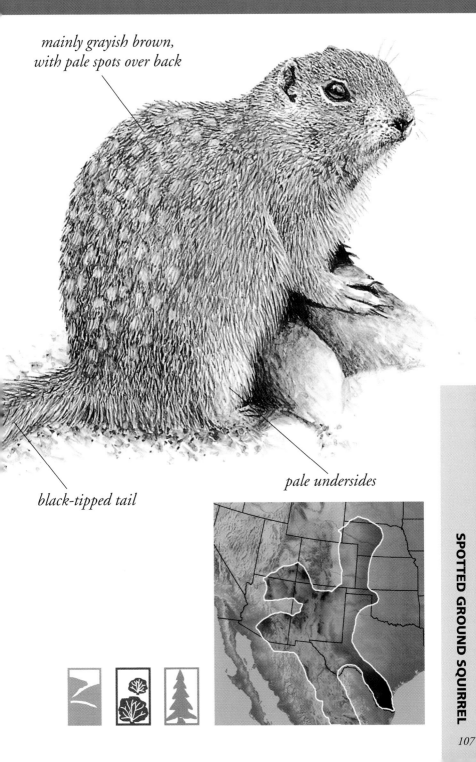

mainly grayish brown,
with pale spots over back

black-tipped tail

pale undersides

Franklin's Ground Squirrel

Spermophilus franklinii

I n the rich, deep-grass prairies of central North America, Franklin's Ground Squirrels appear aboveground in the first weeks of April. Their arrival is marked by their fine, bird-like whistles, which are most frequently heard during their spring mating. Although most members of this genus produce a variety of whistling calls, none rivals the Franklin's Ground Squirrel for clarity and pitch. The spring courtship activities of these squirrels also involves intense fighting between the males. They bump heads and bite each other's rumps, results in nearly every male having a little patch of raw and bleeding flesh near his tail.

Franklin's Ground Squirrels spend half the year in hibernation, and they must build up a heavy layer of fat before beginning their dormancy in October. Almost one-third of their diet is composed of animal protein, a larger portion than most other squirrels. Small vertebrates, such young birds, frogs, mice, duck eggs and carrion are their primary sources of meat. To eat a duck egg, the squirrel rolls the egg underneath its body and then uses its hindlegs to bang the egg against its incisors. The other two-thirds of the diet is seeds, grasses, berries, green vegetation and insects (including larvae).

When they form colonies, Franklin's Ground Squirrels rarely number more than 10 individuals. They make their burrows, both colonial and solitary ones, in the dense grass of open prairies or forest edges. The heavy grass cover limits their view, but also makes them harder to see. These squirrels almost never venture into open, flat country, where they would become easy targets for predation.

ID: grayish-tawny body, with only slightly lighter undersides; black speckling throughout fur; head and tail are brown, with black flecks.

Size: *L* 15–16 in (38–41 cm); *Wt* 18–25 oz (510–710 g).

Habitat: areas of dense grass or brushy cover.

Nesting: burrows.

SIMILAR SPECIES:
Richardson's Ground Squirrel (p. 94) is smaller and has pale undersides. Other ground squirrels in the same range are not as plainly colored.

Richardson's Ground Squirrel

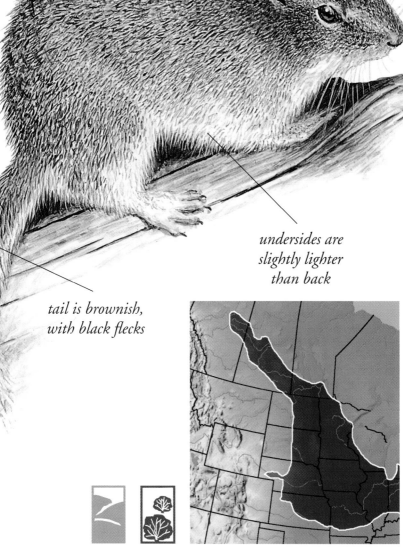

grayish-tawny body

head is brownish,
with black flecks

undersides are
slightly lighter
than back

tail is brownish,
with black flecks

Rock Squirrel

Spermophilus variegatus

This ground squirrel got its name from its preference for rocky landscapes—it makes its burrow underneath large boulders, which provide excellent protection against American Badgers, Coyotes and Bobcats. The Rock Squirrel lives primarily on low cliffs, canyon walls, boulder piles and talus slopes.

With its long, bushy tail, the Rock Squirrel bears a distinct resemblance to the tree squirrels. More so than other ground squirrels, it is an agile climber, and it often climbs through trees to feed on berries or seeds. Its coat is mottled brown and gray, and it has tawny to pink undersides. One of the largest ground squirrels, the Rock Squirrel can reach more than 20 in (51 cm) in length, which is slightly longer than the Columbian Ground Squirrel (p. 86).

Rock Squirrels form large colonies with distinct social orders. Females make their burrows in the center of a colony's territory, while one dominant and a few subordinate males burrow on the outskirts. Like most other ground-dwelling squirrels, Rock Squirrels have a standard whistle that keeps colony members in contact. As well, they have a short, high-pitched alarm squeak, which is followed by a lower-pitched trill.

Ambivalent about dormancy, individual Rock Squirrels may or may not estivate in summer or hibernate in winter. If they estivate, Rock Squirrels are dormant in July and August, the hottest times of the year. Hibernating Rock Squirrels may break their slumber and come aboveground on warmer days. In some parts of their range, Rock Squirrels remain active all year, neither hibernating nor estivating.

ID: dappled, gray-brown body, becoming darker toward tail; buffy-pink undersides; long, bushy tail is mottled brown and gray, with light edging.

Size: *L* 17–21 in (43–53 cm); *Wt* 21–28 oz (600–790 g).

Habitat: rocky outcroppings; cliffs; canyons; talus slopes.

Nesting: burrows in rock crevices.

SIMILAR SPECIES:
California Ground Squirrel (p. 112) is almost as large, but it occurs in a different range. Other ground squirrels in the same range are much smaller.

California Ground Squirrel

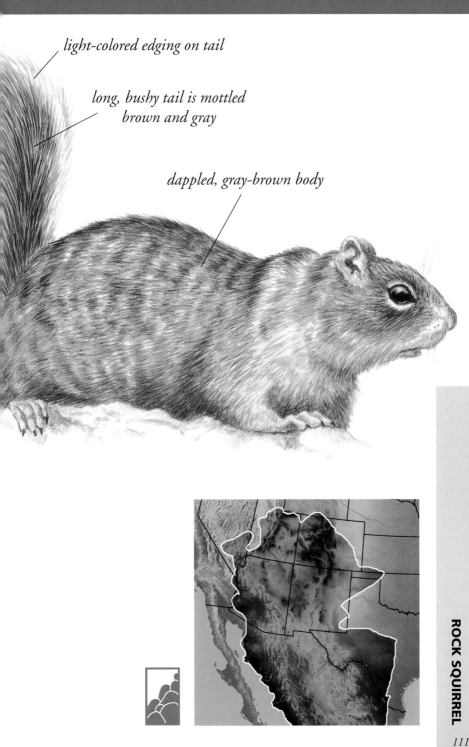

light-colored edging on tail

long, bushy tail is mottled brown and gray

dappled, gray-brown body

California Ground Squirrel

Spermophilus beecheyi

California Ground Squirrels seem antisocial in comparison to most other ground dwellers: they either live alone or in informal colonies. When in colonies, each member respects the living space of the others. Individuals have their own entrances to the colonial burrow, and when a predator approaches, each squirrel scurries for its own entrance, rather than using another squirrel's that might be nearer.

ID: mainly brown; indistinct pale dapples; brownish-gray, bushy tail is edged in white; pale, V-shaped area of fur at neck, running over each shoulder.

Size: L 14–20 in (36–51 cm); Wt 9³/₄–26 oz (280–740 g).

Habitat: pastures and other open areas; rocky outcroppings; rolling hills.

Nesting: burrows.

A good diagnostic feature for this species is the V-shaped pattern of light fur that begins at the nape of the neck and runs over each shoulder to the sides. Otherwise, the California Ground Squirrel is dappled gray or tawny brown, and it has a conspicuously bushy tail that is edged with white.

Like most squirrels, California Ground Squirrels spend a fair portion of each day sunbathing on warm rocks or sand. They cannot tolerate too much heat, however, and before long the hot squirrels retire to their cool burrows.

California Ground Squirrels generally do not estivate, which leaves lots of time for them to fatten their waistlines before they enter hibernation by mid-November. They feed primarily on grains, seeds and green vegetation, although insects and other animal protein may be consumed. Throughout winter, they remain in an unbroken state of dormancy, with their heart rate, metabolism and respiration all slowed. Most of these resourceful squirrels pack a small amount of food into their winter dens so that they have an easy meal waiting for them in spring, when they wake hungry and slim.

SIMILAR SPECIES:
Belding's Ground Squirrel (p. 100) is smaller and lacks the distinctive V-shaped marking at the shoulders.

Belding's Ground Squirrel

white 'V' over shoulders and neck

dark brown inside the 'V'

pale dapples throughout gray or tawny-brown coat

brownish-gray, bushy tail, edged with white

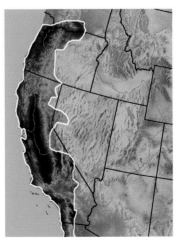

Mohave Ground Squirrel

Spermophilus mohavensis

These small, large-eyed ground squirrels are found only in the Mojave Desert of southern California. To survive in that harsh climate, these little ground squirrels must hibernate almost eight months of the year, from August to March. Food is scarce during those months, and these squirrels are unable to compete for what few morsels are available; they leave that to the White-tailed Antelope Squirrels (p. 76), which also live in the desert and do not hibernate. Mohave Ground Squirrels mainly eat green vegetation, seeds, beans and insects, but they are generalists that will even feed on carrion when it is available.

ID: mainly gray, with pink highlights; very light undersides; thin tail is reddish above and white below.

Size: L 8⁵/₈–9 in (22–23 cm); Wt 3–4⁵/₈ oz (85–131 g).

Habitat: desert regions; brushy flats.

Nesting: burrows.

The Mohave Ground Squirrel has a white belly and a gray coat with a slightly pink glow. Its thin tail is cinnamon colored on top and white underneath. When it runs, the Mohave Ground Squirrel holds its tail over its back to expose the white color, which reflects away some of the sun's harsh rays.

As these mainly solitary ground squirrels excavate their burrows, they scatter the dirt away from the hole to prevent a mound from forming. Without a mound to reveal the entranceway, the burrow can remain well hidden. Like most ground squirrels, Mohave Ground Squirrels adopt an upright, 'bowling pin' stance outside their burrows. In this position, they have a good view of their surroundings and can easily locate approaching predators. If they sense danger, they give a short, high-pitched peep to warn nearby squirrels. The sound sends everyone scurrying to the safety of their burrows. The main predators that threaten Mohave Ground Squirrels are American Badgers, hawks, foxes and Coyotes.

SIMILAR SPECIES:
Round-tailed Ground Squirrel (p. 116) has a longer, solid cinnamon tail.

Round-tailed Ground Squirrel

mainly gray, with pink highlights

very light undersides

thin tail is reddish above and white below

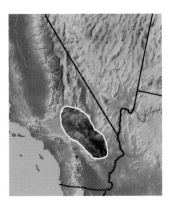

Round-tailed Ground Squirrel

Spermophilus tereticaudus

True to its name, the Round-tailed Ground Squirrel has a long, round-tipped tail. Its tail is thin, as in most other ground squirrels, and it has gray fur on top and cinnamon tones underneath. This squirrel has no special patterns or unique markings in its coat to help with identification: its fur is mainly cinnamon colored or tawny gray. Some of the longer hairs down the sides may be tipped with yellow or light gray, lending a slight sheen to the coat.

Round-tailed Ground Squirrels excavate their burrows in the dry, sandy earth of southern California, Nevada and Arizona. During hot afternoons, they either retire to their cool dens or they climb into scrubby bushes to avoid the burning sand. Although they are excellent diggers, these squirrels often use burrows excavated by other animals, such as pocket gophers or kangaroo rats. When Round-tailed Ground Squirrels are startled, they run for cover by diving into any burrow. Regardless of what might be at home, they would rather take their chances with another burrowing animal than with an American Badger, hawk, Coyote, fox or Bobcat.

These ground squirrels primarily eat seeds, green vegetation, cactus pulp and grasshoppers. Most Round-tailed Ground Squirrels put on enough fat to survive three months of hibernation, which generally lasts from late October to the end of January. Some squirrels living in the more southern regions may not hibernate at all. Round-tailed Ground Squirrels mate in early spring, and by mid-May the female bears a litter of 1 to 12 young, depending entirely on the abundance of water and vegetation.

ID: tawny-cinnamon body with gray highlights; somewhat paler undersides; tail is long and rounded, but not bushy.

Size: *L* 8–11 in (20–28 cm); *Wt* 5–6¹/₂ oz (140–180 g).

Habitat: desert regions; scrub flatlands.

Nesting: burrows.

SIMILAR SPECIES:
Mohave Ground Squirrel (p. 114) is almost identical, but it has a shorter tail that is white underneath, and the fur of its body has pinkish highlights.

Mohave Ground Squirrel

tail is long and rounded, not bushy

tawny-cinnamon body

pale undersides

Golden-mantled Ground Squirrel

(Copperhead)

Spermophilus lateralis

Those playful mountain creatures that stuff themselves on hiker's mix are Golden-mantled Ground Squirrels. When they are not dining on handouts, these squirrels eat a variety of other foods, including seeds, fruits, nuts, mushrooms and assorted vegetation. With their striped backs, these ground squirrels might be mistaken for chipmunks if it were not for their unstriped faces and rotund girths.

ID: tawny gray overall; reddish shoulders and face; whitish undersides; 1 cream-colored stripe down each side, bordered by 2 black stripes.

Size: *L* 9–12 in (23–30 cm); *Wt* 6–9³/4 oz (170–280 g).

Habitat: coniferous and mixed forests; rocky slopes; sometimes open shrubby land.

Nesting: burrows; rock crevices.

In late summer and fall, Golden-mantled Ground Squirrels put on a heavy layer of fat to sustain them through hibernation. As an extra measure of security, they store food in their winter dens, using their cheek pouches to carry it in. The stored food will support them when they first wake in spring, and also if they wake up during winter. Hibernating squirrels can be roused by either unusually warm or unusually cold winter weather—a ground squirrel may wake up during severely cold temperatures to raise its body temperature enough to prevent freezing to death. While awake, a squirrel will partake of a sizable meal from its pantry before retreating into dormancy again.

Golden-mantled Ground Squirrels are less sociable than other ground-dwelling squirrels. Too concerned with eating and hoarding food, they usually ignore each other. Males and females are seen together in spring, during courtship, but after mating the males leave and the females raise their young alone.

SIMILAR SPECIES:
Cascade Golden-mantled Ground Squirrel (p. 120) is visually very similar but occupies a different range. All chipmunks (pp. 12–57) are smaller and have striped faces.

Cascade Golden-mantled Ground Squirrel

tawny appearance
overall

reddish shoulders
and face

one cream-colored stripe,
bordered by two black
stripes, down each side

short brown
tail

Cascade Golden-mantled Ground Squirrel

Spermophilus saturatus

Living in the Cascade Mountains of southern British Columbia and central Washington is the Cascade Golden-mantled Ground Squirrel. This striped squirrel is similar in appearance to the Golden-mantled Ground Squirrel (p. 118), but it has less distinct stripes. Its overall color is rich chestnut brown, with a clear, pale stripe down each side of the back, indistinctly bordered with darker fur. The Golden-mantled Ground Squirrel has dark black fur bordering the pale stripes.

Cascade Golden-mantled Ground Squirrels feed on a wide variety of foods in their mountain homes, but they favor huckleberry, lupine and mountain ash seeds and berries, green vegetation, bark and subterranean fungi. Eating heartily of these foods during their active period, which lasts from mid-March to mid-August, they can more than double their weight before entering their eight-month hibernation. Some individuals (mostly males) may attempt to postpone hibernation until as late as mid-September. Those that do are an ill-fated bunch, however, because predation takes the majority of them. The major predators of Cascade Golden-mantled Ground Squirrels are owls, hawks, eagles, foxes and weasels.

ID: dark brown overall; red in face and shoulders; 1 pale stripe down each side, indistinctly bordered by 2 darker stripes.

Size: L 11–12 in (28–30 cm); Wt 7–10 oz (200–280 g).

Habitat: various habitats, including open coniferous forests and talus slopes at and below treeline.

Nesting: burrows.

This ground squirrel has a distant cousin, the Yellow-pine Chipmunk (p. 20), that shares the same habitat. The two species appear to feed on the same foods and burrow in the same areas, but they manage to avoid direct competition: slight differences in their specific niches allow these two squirrels to live together harmoniously.

SIMILAR SPECIES:
Golden-mantled Ground Squirrel (p. 118) has clearer stripes on the sides, and the dark stripes are nearly black.

Golden-mantled Ground Squirrel

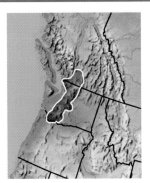

*one pale stripe,
indistinctly bordered by
two darker stripes,
down each side*

*dark brown
overall*

*reddish face and
shoulders*

CASCADE GOLDEN-MANTLED GROUND SQUIRREL

Prairie-Dogs

Of the ground dwellers, the most gregarious are the prairie-dogs, which are found exclusively in North America. They live in family groups, large colonies or immense 'towns' that can number up to thousands of individuals, as is the case with the Black-tailed Prairie-Dog. Prairie-dog burrows vary in complexity, depending on the particular species and the size of the colony, but, in general, prairie-dogs excavate more intricate burrow systems than any other squirrels.

Over the last 100 years, prairie-dogs have experienced population explosions and near extinction—they have been both persecuted and celebrated. When the bison were killed in the prairies to make room for agriculture and cattle grazing, prairie-dog populations exploded. Unwittingly, prairie-dogs graze on the same grass that cattle do, and ranchers soon realized that 250 of these squirrels eat as much in one day as one full-grown steer. Extermination programs nearly drove the four species of prairie-dogs to extinction. The plight of the Black-footed Ferret, one the most endangered mammals in North America, is a result of the near-extinction of prairie-dogs, its primary food source.

As their name suggests, prairie-dogs are generally thought of as prairie animals, but some species are quite comfortable living in grassy mountain regions. These ground dwellers feed primarily on seeds, roots and green vegetation.

connection to rest of 'town'

Black-tailed Prairie-Dog performing
leap-squeak display

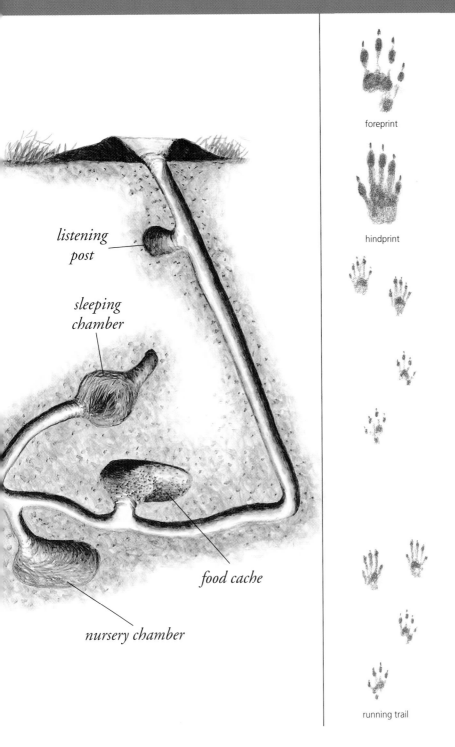

listening
post

sleeping
chamber

food cache

nursery chamber

foreprint

hindprint

running trail

123

Black-tailed Prairie-Dog

Cynomys ludovicianus

Black-tailed Prairie-Dogs are one of the curiosities of prairie regions: living in prairie-dogs towns that can number several thousand individuals, these squirrels are among the most gregarious of all North American mammals. Their colonies are so large that there are community subdivisions within a town. Each community is composed of a dominant male, a few females and an assortment of yearlings and babies. Each community has a defensible territory, and each member is responsible to call the alarm if it detects a predator approaching its boundaries.

When community members cross paths, they first touch noses and then turn their heads to touch incisors. Prairie-dogs use this greeting as a gesture of recognition and welcome between neighbors. Community members routinely groom each other, a behavior that helps strengthen the social bonds in a colony.

The complex, intertwined burrows of Black-tailed Prairie-Dogs are a remarkable feat of engineering. A prairie-dog town has thousands of branches and rooms, including sleeping chambers, excrement chambers and listening posts. The listening posts are located about 3 ft (91 cm) inside a tunnel, and they allow an individual to keep tabs on a lurking predator, such as the elusive Black-footed Ferret, from the safety of the burrow. When all is clear, the prairie-dogs leap from their burrows and run around in a playful, noisy display. They throw their heads back and leap into the air while wheezing a high-pitched squeak. This behavior is contagious, and soon all the prairie-dogs have emerged to join in the leap-squeak display.

ID: mainly tawny pink in color; lighter undersides; black-tipped tail; small ears.

Size: *L* 14–16 in (36–41 cm); *Wt* 32–48 oz (910–1360 g).

Habitat: shortgrass prairies.

Nesting: burrow 'towns.'

SIMILAR SPECIES:
White-tailed (p. 126), Utah (p. 128) and Gunnison's (p. 130) prairie-dogs are smaller, have white-tipped tails and live in smaller colonies.

White-tailed Prairie-Dog

small ears

tawny or
slightly pinkish
upperparts

black-
tipped tail

light undersides

White-tailed Prairie-Dog

Cynomys leucurus

Easily identified by their white-tipped tails, these prairie-dogs occur in great numbers in the sagebrush plains of Utah, Wyoming and Colorado. White-tailed Prairie-Dog burrows are marked with large mounds of dirt that can be up to 3 ft (91 cm) high and 9 ft (2.7 m) across. Because of their extremely large size, however, the mounds may be overlooked as entranceways to the prairie-dog town.

White-tailed Prairie-Dogs are less sociable than Black-tailed Prairie-Dogs (p. 124): they live in smaller colonies and spend less time engaged in grooming and 'kissing' behaviors. Unlike their black-tailed cousins, they do not engage in cooperative excavation projects to link each burrow to its neighbors. For safety and social order, these prairie-dogs may excavate just a few links in the passageways of their town.

White-tailed Prairie-Dogs live at high, cool elevations where winters can be cold and long, so these ground dwellers must hibernate. Their dormancy is uninterrupted, and they sleep straight through from late October to March. When they emerge from hibernation after a long winter, they are slim and hungry, but after a few good meals of spring seedlings, these prairie-dogs are ready to mate. Their gestation is about 30 days, after which about five blind, hairless and helpless babies are born. From the time that they emerge from their burrows in spring until they re-enter dormancy in late fall, White-tailed Prairie-Dogs must at least double their body weight. Over the course of the summer, they fatten themselves on grasses and herbaceous plants; by October, their bellies wax large and they become steadily lazier.

ID: robust prairie-dog; mainly tawny pink in color; somewhat paler below; short tail with white terminal half; darks patches above and below eyes.

Size: *L* 13–15 in (33–38 cm); *Wt* 24–40 oz (680–1130 g).

Habitat: sagebrush and grassland plains at high elevations.

Nesting: burrow 'towns.'

SIMILAR SPECIES:
Gunnison's Prairie-Dog (p. 130) has gray on the terminal half of the tail. Black-tailed Prairie-Dog (p. 124) has a black-tipped tail. Utah Prairie-Dog (p. 128) is redder.

Black-tailed Prairie-Dog

dark patches above
and below eyes

tawny-pink coat

terminal
half of tail
is entirely
white

pale undersides

WHITE-TAILED PRAIRIE-DOG

Utah Prairie-Dog

Cynomys parvidens

On the shortgrass prairies of Utah, small towns of the threatened Utah Prairie-Dog can be found. The ideal location to observe these rare creatures is the Packer Mountain area in south-central Utah. Occurring nowhere else in the world, this ground dweller is a close relative of the White-tailed Prairie-Dog (p. 126). Many biologists consider the Utah Prairie-Dog to be a subspecies of the White-tailed, but the two live in distinct populations, and it has never been shown that they interbreed.

The Utah Prairie-Dog has tawny to brick brown fur, mixed with black-tipped hairs, whereas the White-tailed Prairie-Dog has yellow to pinkish-gray fur flecked with black. Also, the dark eyebrow on the Utah Prairie-Dog is neither as dark nor as distinct as the White-tail's eyebrow. These two species have similar habits, and both are colonial, but the Utah Prairie-Dog typically lives in smaller colonies. Prairie-dog towns are a favorite hunting ground for several predators, such as rattlesnakes and Burrowing Owls, which both prey on young prairie-dogs.

ID: tawny-red fur, mixed with black-tipped hairs; paler undersides; white-tipped tail; somewhat darker fur above and below eyes.

Size: *L* 12–14 in (30–36 cm); *Wt* 24–38 oz (680–1080 g).

Habitat: shortgrass prairies.

Nesting: burrow 'towns.'

During the massive efforts to exterminate prairie-dogs that occurred over the last 100 years, the Utah Prairie-Dog came very close to extinction. Recently, a better understanding of rangeland and ecosystems has resulted in many ranchers actively protecting prairie-dog towns. A balanced population of plants and animals, including prairie-dogs, which aerate and turn over soil, improves the quality of valued rangeland. Unfortunately, the Utah Prairie-Dog has not rebounded as successfully as its relatives since the cessation of the fierce extermination efforts; its numbers, much reduced, may still be fewer than 5000 individuals.

SIMILAR SPECIES:
White-tailed Prairie-Dog (p. 126) appears pinker. Black-tailed Prairie-Dog (p. 124) has a black-tipped tail. Gunnison's Prairie-Dog (p. 130) has gray in the terminal half of its tail.

White-tailed Prairie-Dog

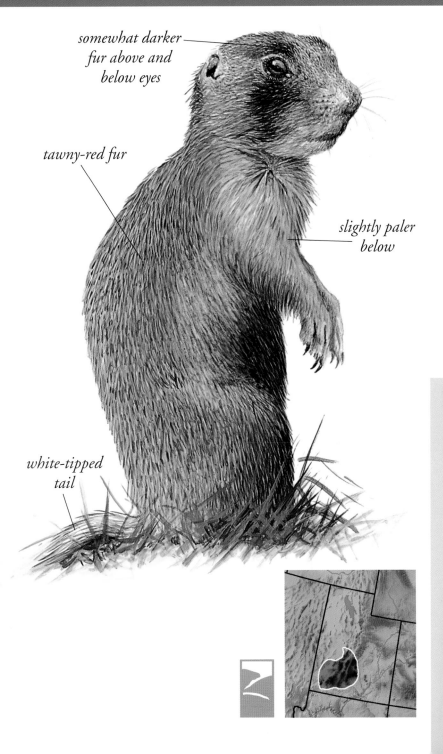

somewhat darker fur above and below eyes

tawny-red fur

slightly paler below

white-tipped tail

Gunnison's Prairie-Dog

Cynomys gunnisoni

Their high-pitched barks and bubbly chatter give away the presence of Gunnison's Prairie-Dogs. Living on the high grassland slopes and plateaus of the southern Rocky Mountains, these prairie-dogs behave more like ground squirrels than other member of their genus. While some prairie-dog species live in extremely large towns, Gunnison's Prairie-Dogs generally live in colonies of only about 50 individuals. The size of a colony is strongly affected by the surroundings: in flatter habitats, colonies can be much larger because each member of the group can see the others, which strengthens the safety of the colony and maintains hierarchies; in less desirable habitats, such as shrubby terrain or rolling hills, increased predation and a lack of suitable burrowing ground prevents large colonies from forming. Human encroachment on these squirrels' preferred territory has pushed them further into marginal habitats.

ID: tawny yellow in color; black flecks throughout coat; slightly paler undersides; white-tipped tail, with silvery patch on terminal half.

Size: *L* 12–15 in (30–38 cm); *Wt* 23–42 oz (650–1190 g).

Habitat: shortgrass prairies at high elevations.

Nesting: burrow 'towns.'

The Gunnison's Prairie-Dog's extensive burrows are less complex and shallower than the burrows of the more common Black-tailed Prairie-Dog (p. 124). Each burrow has only one nest chamber and is without food or waste alcoves—these prairie-dogs eat and defecate outside. The Gunnison's Prairie-Dog excavates its burrows on slightly sloped land to maximize drainage. Unlike other prairie-dogs, it does not tamp the excavated dirt into a mound at the entrance to the burrow, nor does it remove grass and weeds that sprout near the opening. Loose rocks, grass tufts and scattered dirt disguise the whereabouts of this prairie-dog's home.

Active only during the day, Gunnison's Prairie-Dogs are routinely seen feeding, grooming and playing. In their high-elevation homes, they feed primarily on grasses, forbs, shrubs and insects. These squirrels hibernate for several months during winter, so they must build up a layer of fat through summer.

Black-tailed Prairie-Dog

SIMILAR SPECIES:
Black-tailed Prairie-Dog (p. 124) has a black-tipped tail. White-tailed Prairie-Dog (p. 126) and Utah Prairie-Dog (p. 128) have white, rather than silver gray, on the terminal half of the tail.

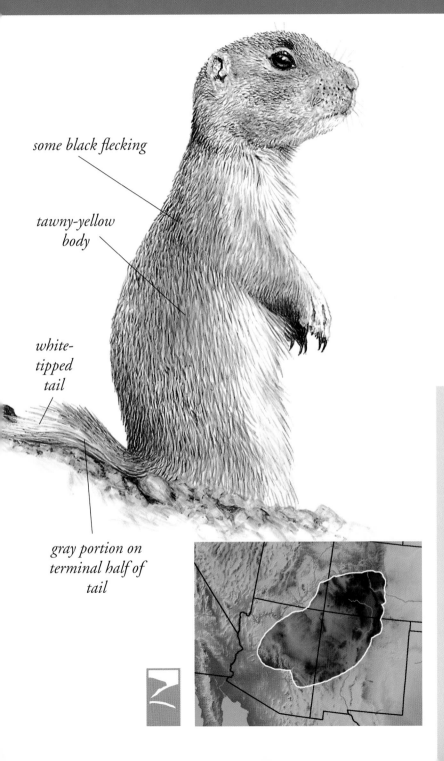

some black flecking

tawny-yellow
body

white-
tipped
tail

gray portion on
terminal half of
tail

Tree Squirrels

Agile and sure-footed, tree squirrels are common inhabitants of treed regions throughout North America. Tree squirrels are divided into two genera: the large grayish squirrels (*Sciurus*) and the smaller reddish squirrels (*Tamiasciurus*). The scientific name *Sciurus* comes from the Greek words *skia*, meaning 'shadow,' and *oura*, meaning 'tail'—when tree squirrels run through the trees, they frequently stop and lay their long tails over their backs, providing shade in summer and warmth in winter.

Tree squirrels are highly specialized for arboreal life: they typically have larger eyes and ears than their ground-dwelling relatives, as well as longer, bushier tails to better balance in the treetops. Unlike ground squirrels and chipmunks, tree squirrels have no cheek pouches for storing and carrying food, and they don't have any stripes on their backs.

Using their well-muscled hindlegs for leaping and their curved claws for clinging, these squirrels rely on trees for shelter and food, and for the maze of transportation routes formed by the branches. In true sciurid fashion, tree squirrels feed on conifer seeds, nuts, fruits, green vegetation, mushrooms, insects and occasionally other animals. All the tree squirrels are non-hibernating, and in northern regions they must store enormous amounts of food to survive winter. They den in leafy tree nests, called 'dreys,' in tree cavities or, less frequently, in burrows dug inside their middens.

Red Squirrel defending its midden

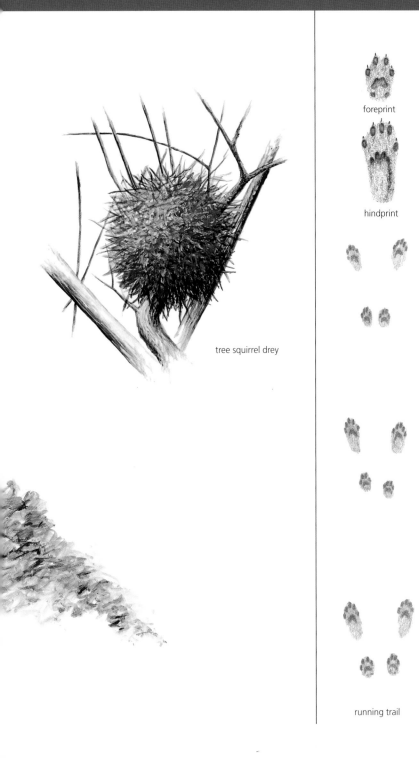

foreprint

hindprint

tree squirrel drey

running trail

Eastern Gray Squirrel

Sciurus carolinensis

The Eastern Gray Squirrel is the most frequently encountered large squirrel in eastern North America. It is active throughout the entire year, sometimes even digging through snow to retrieve its buried nuts. West of the Mississippi, this squirrel's natural range extends into the eastern fringes of the Great Plains. The western occurrence of this species is increasing, however, and introduced populations are thriving in Vancouver, Seattle and Calgary.

Many stories are told of great migrations of Eastern Gray Squirrels. Although they migrate infrequently, they may journey in response to food and population stresses. If a year of abundant food and high reproduction rates is followed by a year of little food, thousands of these squirrels may migrate great distances to find new food sources. When these squirrels travel, they cover large tracks of forests without ever touching the ground.

The mainstay diet for these squirrels is nuts and seeds. An individual Eastern Gray Squirrel will have dozens of nut caches buried just under the surface of the soil. While the caches of most other squirrels germinate if left for too long, Eastern Gray Squirrels determinedly nip off the germinating end of the nuts before burying them. These squirrels routinely travel throughout their home range, keeping apprised of the fresh food sources available. Their caches of nuts are security for winter and stormy days; fresh corn crops, flowers, fruits and mushrooms are relished when they are available.

ID: medium-sized squirrel; mainly gray upperparts; pale gray undersides; bushy, flattened tail; backs of ears are light colored; reddish-brown tail and belly is common in northern areas; black forms are common.

Size: *L* 17–20 in (43–51 cm); *Wt* 14–25 oz (400–710 g).

Habitat: deciduous hardwood and mixed forests.

Nesting: spherical, leafy tree nests; tree cavities.

The Eastern Gray Squirrel has two distinct color forms: most adults are dusty gray overall, with pale undersides and a silvery, flattened tail; occasionally, a solid ebony black form of this squirrel is encountered. In Canada, the gray form often has cinnamon highlights on the head, back and tail. Some local populations, such as the one in Calgary, are almost entirely black.

SIMILAR SPECIES:
Eastern Fox Squirrel (p. 136) is larger and has yellowish highlights throughout its coat.

all-black form of
Eastern Gray Squirrel

*bushy tail may be
reddish brown*

*backsides of ears are
light colored*

*head may have cinnamon
or reddish highlights*

*mainly gray
upperparts*

*light gray to white
undersides*

Eastern Fox Squirrel

Sciurus niger

The largest and most colorful of the tree squirrels, the Eastern Fox Squirrel comes in three different color forms: in the northeastern part of its range, it is dusty gray with yellowish undersides; moving west, its undersides become bright tawny red; in southern regions, it is mainly black, with a silvery rump and tail and a white blaze on the face. Only the latter two forms occur west of the Mississippi.

ID: largest tree squirrel; 2 western color phases: mainly gray with orange to red-brown undersides in north, and black-and-gray with white blaze on face and white-tipped tail in south.

Size: *L* 18–28 in (46–71 cm); *Wt* 18–38 oz (510–1080 g).

Habitat: forested regions of all types.

Nesting: spherical, leafy tree nests; tree cavities.

Eastern Fox Squirrels usually lead solitary lives, but in areas where food is plentiful, many of these squirrels aggregate together to feed. They collect seeds, fruits, fungi, green pine cones and corn. They bury any non-perishables, such as seeds and nuts, in caches just under the ground surface. Their most gregarious behavior occurs in winter, when several adults whose home ranges overlap, and who are often related, share food caches and tree cavities. Eastern Fox Squirrels remain active in winter, and the individuals sharing a tree cavity come and go regardless of the cold. The sharing that occurs between Eastern Fox Squirrels is not as sociable as the behavior seen in ground squirrels: fox squirrels do not groom each other, 'kiss' or nuzzle to maintain friendly ties.

Where tree cavities are scarce, fox squirrels build medium-sized tree nests. Just over 1 ft (30 cm) wide, the nests are spherical masses of leaves and twigs built in tree forks high off the ground. The nest materials are taken from the tree in which they are built. Green and leafy, the nests are hard to distinguish amid the foliage. Throughout their home range, mature squirrels usually maintain three to six dens, either in tree cavities or leaf nests.

SIMILAR SPECIES:
Eastern Gray Squirrel (p. 134) is smaller and has a frosty appearance.

southern form of Eastern Fox Squirrel

mainly gray fur

*orange to
red-brown
undersides*

*underside of tail is
tawny orange*

northern form of Eastern Fox Squirrel

Mexican Fox Squirrel
(Chiricahua Squirrel, Apache Squirrel, Nayarit Squirrel)

Sciurus nayaritensis

This colorful tree squirrel is found only in the Chiricahua Mountains of southeastern Arizona. A close relative of the Eastern Fox Squirrel (p. 136), the Mexican Fox Squirrel is the only large squirrel in its range. Easy to recognize, it is gray with ochre undersides. Freshly gnawed Douglas-fir cones are a sure sign that one of these squirrels is nearby.

ID: mainly gray body with ochre undersides; often has yellow highlights throughout coat.

Size: L 21–23 in (53–58 cm); Wt 18–38 oz (510–1080 g).

Habitat: coniferous and deciduous wooded areas.

Nesting: tree cavities; spherical leaf nests.

Although they favor conifer cones, Mexican Fox Squirrels vary their diet with walnuts and acorns—they live in mixedwood forests of pine, oak and walnut, each of which provide food and shelter for the squirrels. Most of the cones and nuts they collect are stashed in tree hollows or buried about $1/2$ in (1.3 cm) under the soil surface to be eaten later.

Mexican Fox Squirrels den in either leaf nests or tree cavities, which are lined on the inside with comfortable bits of dry grass and leaves. Tree cavities afford more warmth and protection to the squirrels, and they are favored by expectant mothers. About 45 days after mating, a female bears two to four young in the safety of a cavity nest. Adult females bear at least one litter a year, anytime from late February to early September, although spring is most common. Older females may bear a second litter in summer.

Mexican Fox Squirrels are active throughout the entire year. They are not colonial, but they are occasionally seen in large aggregations where food is plentiful.

Eastern Fox Squirrel

SIMILAR SPECIES:
Eastern Fox Squirrel (p. 136) may appear similar, but it occurs much further east.

long, gray, bushy tail

mainly gray body

ochre undersides

Arizona Gray Squirrel

Sciurus arizonensis

Found only in scattered regions of Arizona, the Arizona Gray Squirrel is a close relative of the Eastern Gray Squirrel (p. 134). Similar in appearance to the ground-dwelling Rock Squirrel (p. 110), this tree squirrel is plain gray overall, with pale flecking over its back. Its long tail is fringed with white, which helps flag its whereabouts in dense forests.

Arizona Gray Squirrels live primarily in deciduous forests of walnut, sycamore and poplar trees. They build their nests high up in the fork of a tree, where it is visible only in the leafless winter. The nests are typically spherical in shape and are made of dry leaves and twigs. Like other tree squirrels, Arizona Gray Squirrels do not hibernate; their nests are used only for sleeping and as refuges in times of danger. Sometimes rickety nests can be found, which is an unusual occurrence for such good builders. These ramshackle nests are built either by unpracticed juveniles or as temporary lodgings close to a favored food source.

ID: plain gray overall; white undersides; long gray tail is fringed with white.

Size: *L* 20–22 in (51–56 cm); *Wt* 22–25 oz (620–710 g).

Habitat: mainly deciduous lowland forests.

Nesting: leafy tree nests; tree cavities.

Adults mate anytime between January and June. Females are only receptive for a short while, and they have only one litter a year. A female who is ready to mate attracts at least one male, who follows her everywhere she goes. Sometimes called a 'chase,' the courtship game is more like 'follow-the-leader,' because the male imitates everything she does. After about six weeks of gestation, a female bears two or three young. The tiny squirrels are entirely dependent on their mother for nourishment and care during their first six weeks. When they are seven weeks old, the youngsters are weaned and soon disperse.

SIMILAR SPECIES:
Abert's Squirrel (p. 144) is also gray, but it has distinctive ear tufts and a broadly plumed tail.

Abert's Squirrel

long, gray tail, fringed with white

gray body

nearly white
undersides

Western Gray Squirrel
(California Gray Squirrel)
Sciurus griseus

The Western Gray Squirrel is a common resident throughout the West Coast. This large tree squirrel is mainly smoky gray, but it has white and cinnamon highlights. It has white undersides and a long, broadly plumed tail.

These arboreal squirrels are comfortable at great heights in the humid western forests. Intermingling tree branches are like highways to these squirrels, allowing them to cover great distances without ever touching the ground. Their nests are at least 20 ft (6.1 m) off the ground, and often near the tops of tall trees. Such heights effectively remove them from the reach of many carnivores.

During summer, Western Gray Squirrels build nests that are similar to those of other tree squirrels. The spherical nests are made from twigs, bark and dry leaves, and they can measure more than 2 ft (61 cm) in diameter. In winter, they ignore their now visible leafy nests and take up lodging in a tree cavity instead. Tree cavities tend to be warmer, as well as more secret, which helps the squirrel stay warm in case of extremely cold weather. Western Gray Squirrels do not hibernate; instead, they remain active during daytime hours for the entire year. Like all squirrels, they prefer mild weather and will not leave their nests during stormy conditions.

When searching for food, Western Gray Squirrels travel in trees and on the ground. They look for pine cones, nuts, berries, insects and fungi. Many of the seeds and nuts they collect are stashed away for later use. They make their caches in forked tree branches, under fallen logs or buried in the ground. When they forget about a food cache, the seeds germinate and replenish the plants on which they feed.

ID: large gray squirrel with many white-tipped hairs throughout coat; white undersides; some red tones behind ears; long, broadly plumed tail is banded with white, gray and black.

Size: *L* 18–23 in (46–58 cm); *Wt* 12–34 oz (340–960 g).

Habitat: forested regions.

Nesting: mainly spherical leaf nests; tree cavities in winter.

SIMILAR SPECIES:
Northern Flying Squirrel (p. 154) is smaller and has distinctive 'flight' membranes. Douglas's Squirrel (p. 148) is smaller and browner.

Northern Flying Squirrel

tail has banded appearance, from hairs that have black bases, gray middles and white tips

mainly gray, with many white-tipped hairs

white undersides

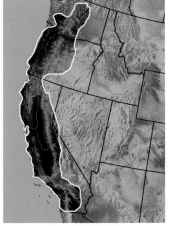

Abert's Squirrel
(Tassel-eared Squirrel)
Sciurus aberti

The Abert's Squirrel, which lives in coniferous forests of the southernmost Rocky Mountains, is easy to identify: it has long ear tufts and a broadly plumed tail that are conspicuous even in dense forests. This squirrel is mainly gray, but it has a brown stripe running down its back, and a black stripe on each side separates its gray upperparts from its pale undersides. Its luxurious white tail is gray on top. One rare subspecies of the Abert's Squirrel is the 'Kaibab Squirrel,' which has a totally white tail and lives only on the north rim of the Grand Canyon.

Abert's Squirrels build spherical tree nests out of twigs and leaves. They are accomplished architects, and some of the nests can measure almost 3 ft (91 cm) in diameter. On occasion, these squirrels make nests in the matted clumps of pine twigs that occur naturally when a pine tree is infected with mistletoe. The squirrels hollow out these clumps and stuff them with soft leaves for bedding. Abert's Squirrels do not hibernate in winter: very cold winter weather may keep them in their nests, but they do not enter a dormant state. These squirrels use their nests as refuges during the day and for sleeping at night.

Abert's Squirrels find and store food throughout the year. They feed primarily on the seeds and inner bark of ponderosa pine, on piñon nuts and on an assortment of other vegetation. They do not store food in their nests; instead they prefer to bury their collections nearby. As is true for most squirrels, they sometimes forget where their caches are, resulting in the germination of the buried seeds.

ID: large, mainly dark gray squirrel, sometimes with reddish highlights over back; white undersides; long, broadly plumed and white-tipped tail; ears have long gray tufts, shorter in summer.

Size: *L* 18–23 in (46–58 cm); *Wt* 24–32 oz (680–910 g).

Habitat: mainly coniferous forests.

Nesting: spherical, leafy nests; tree cavities.

SIMILAR SPECIES:
Arizona Gray Squirrel (p. 140) doesn't have ear tufts. Red Squirrel (p. 146) is smaller and redder.

'Kaibab Squirrel'

long, gray ear tufts

mainly dark gray

sometimes has reddish highlights over back

broadly plumed, white-tipped tail

Red Squirrel
(Chickaree, Pine Squirrel)
Tamiasciurus hudsonicus

F ew squirrels have earned such a reputation for playfulness and roguery as the Red Squirrel. This squirrel is a well-known backyard and ravine inhabitant that often has a saucy regard for its human neighbors. A Red Squirrel will firmly scold all intruders with shrill chatters, clucks and sputters, falsettos, tail flicking and feet stamping. Even when it is undisturbed, this chatterbox often chirps as it goes about its daily routine.

For this industrious squirrel, the daytime hours are devoted almost entirely to food gathering and storage. Red Squirrels urgently collect fir, spruce and pine cones, mushrooms, fruits and seeds in preparation for the winter months. Because Red Squirrels do not hibernate, they need to store massive winter food caches. They remain active throughout winter, except in severely cold weather. At temperatures below −13° F (−25° C) the squirrels stay warm, but awake, in their nests.

By the end of winter, Red Squirrels are ready to mate. Their courtship involves daredevil leaps through the trees and chases over the forest floor. Between the months of April and June, two to seven pink, blind babies are born. The youngsters are playful and frequently challenge nuts or mushrooms to aggressive mortal combat.

The smallest of the tree squirrels, Red Squirrels are distinguished by their rusty red coats, creamy undersides and white eye rings. Like most tree squirrels, they live in any of three types of nests: old woodpecker holes, refurbished corvid nests or ground nests that are dug under stumps or inside their middens. Red Squirrels frequently have mites and insects living along with them in their nests, despite their frequent grooming.

ID: reddish-brown coat and creamy undersides, separated by black side stripe; red tail; white eye ring.

Size: *L* 11–15 in (28–38 cm); *Wt* 5–8⅞ oz (140–250 g).

Habitat: almost any forest; city parks; ravines.

Nesting: tree cavities; leafy twig nests; refurbished corvid nests; burrows.

SIMILAR SPECIES:
Douglas's Squirrel (p. 148) is not as red and has tawnier undersides.

Douglas's Squirrel

red tail

reddish-brown
coat

white eye ring

cream-colored
undersides

Douglas's Squirrel

Tamiasciurus douglasii

Famous for having large repertoires of calls and noisy lifestyles, Douglas's Squirrels are frequently-heard denizens of the West Coast. These squirrels are closely related to Red Squirrels (p. 146), and the two are sometimes difficult to tell apart. The most notable difference between them is the color of their undersides: Red Squirrels have cream-colored bellies; Douglas's Squirrels are yellow-gray to pumpkin orange underneath. Also, Douglas's Squirrels are colored warm brown on their backs, with gray highlights; Red Squirrels have rust-colored backs.

Living almost exclusively in coniferous forests, Douglas's Squirrels leap easily from limb to limb as they search for food. Although they eat green vegetation, acorns, mushrooms and fruits, Douglas's Squirrels are renowned for their appetite for conifer cones. Running along conifer branches, they nip the cones free and let them fall to the ground. On a busy day, these squirrels bombard the forest floor with cone pellets for much of the morning. When enough cones have been cut, the squirrels eagerly transfer them to large cone caches beside tree stumps or under fallen logs.

Douglas's Squirrels are diurnal and are active throughout the entire year. They build nests twice a year, sometimes refurbishing a prior year's nest. Their summer nests are high up in tree branches and look like balls of moss, twigs, lichens and shredded bark. In winter, they find suitable tree cavities that provide shelter from cold winds. Females have a least one litter a year, in spring, and perhaps a second one in autumn. They bear their four to six young inside a tree cavity nest.

ID: mainly chestnut brown, with dull, tawny-orange undersides; black stripe separates brown back from lighter belly; dark-tipped tail is often edged with fine, pale hairs.

Size: *L* 11–14 in (28–36 cm); *Wt* 5¼–11 oz (150–310 g).

Habitat: mainly coniferous forests.

Nesting: spherical, leafy twig nests; tree cavities; old bird nests.

SIMILAR SPECIES:
Red Squirrel (p. 146) is redder overall and has cream-colored undersides.

Red Squirrel

dark-tipped tail may be edged with fine white hairs

mainly chestnut brown

black stripe separates brown back from lighter belly

tawny-orange undersides

Flying Squirrels

Contrary to their name, flying squirrels do not actually fly, but they do possess one of the most unique adaptations of the squirrel family. When a flying squirrel leaps from a tree, its flattened body and lateral skin folds allow it to glide for great distances—sometimes more than 150 ft (46 m)—to search for food, to find a mate or to escape predators.

Flying squirrels are unique in the squirrel family, not only because they are able to 'fly,' but also because they are the only squirrels that prefer the nighttime hours. Their large eyes, brown to steel gray fur, light undersides and vibrissae (whiskers) are characteristics well-suited to nocturnal activity. Any predator looking up at a flying squirrel at night would have difficulty distinguishing the white-bellied squirrel against a moonlit sky, and viewing the dark backs of these squirrels from above is equally ineffective.

Emerging from their nests in the evening, flying squirrels climb high into the trees and leap into the air. Once airborne, they reach out with their arms and legs, and the furred, membranous skin that normally hangs loose at their sides is stretched taut. Flying squirrels are full of grace and agility when airborne—they can make rapid side-to-side maneuvers and tight downward spirals with minor adjustments in the orientation of their wrists and arms—but they are awkward on the ground. Living almost entirely in trees, they feed on seeds, fruits, insects and other animals. They make their homes both in tree cavities and in leafy twig nests, and their calls are chirping and bird-like, often resembling those of the night-flying warblers with which they share the forests.

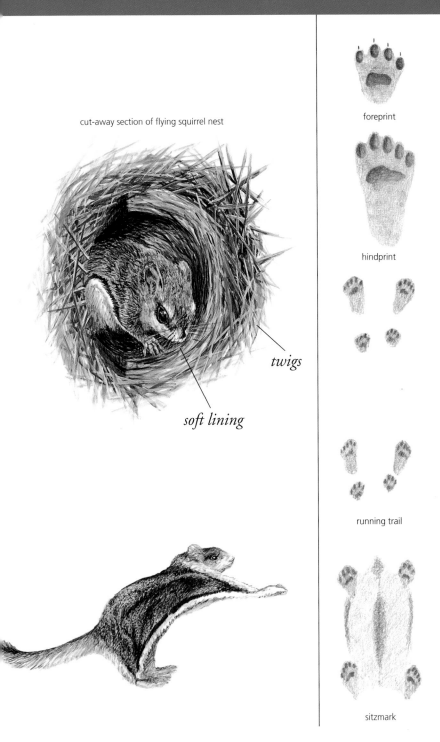

cut-away section of flying squirrel nest

twigs

soft lining

foreprint

hindprint

running trail

sitzmark

Southern Flying Squirrel

Glaucomys volans

S mall and steel gray, the Southern Flying Squirrel is a common denizen of eastern forests. It is active after sunset and just before morning, however, so very few people ever see this striking squirrel. Flying squirrels cannot 'fly' without trees, and this southern species is stopped at the eastern edge of the Great Plains—its range extends only as far west as Minnesota in the north and eastern Texas in the south.

When a flying squirrel leaps from a tree, it stretches out its arms and legs to pull its glide membranes taut, and it is airborne. Just before crashing into its target—usually another tree trunk or branch—it drops its tail low and lifts its shoulders. This action slackens the glide membranes, which now serve as a parachute to slow the squirrel's descent. The squirrel lands gently on its feet and quickly scampers to the other side of the branch, just in case a predator was watching its flight.

Other than its ability to glide and its nocturnal activity, which it shares with its northern counterpart, the Southern Flying Squirrel leads the life of a regular tree squirrel. It collects and eats nuts, seeds, fruits, mushrooms and insects. Its taste for meat is perhaps stronger than that of other squirrels: it regularly eats small vertebrates and carrion.

Although the Southern Flying Squirrel is primarily non-hibernating, severe winter conditions may induce a metabolic torpor in some individuals. This torpid state outwardly resembles hibernation, but it is short lived and not as deep. After the cold snap has passed, a torpid squirrel rouses and resumes activity. Huddling is a more common response to cold weather than torpor—in winter, 5 to 50 flying squirrels are often found together in a tree cavity, relying on their body temperatures to warm the den space.

ID: small squirrel; fine, cool gray coat, sometimes with cinnamon highlights; white undersides; black-edged glide membranes between fore and hind legs; broadly plumed, flattened tail.

Size: L $7^3/4$–10 in (20–25 cm); Wt $1^1/2$–$3^1/2$ oz (43–99 g).

Habitat: deciduous forests, especially beech-maple and oak-hickory.

Nesting: refurbished corvid nests; spherical, leafy tree nests; tree cavities.

SIMILAR SPECIES:
Northern Flying Squirrel (p. 154) is larger and often browner.

Northern Flying Squirrel

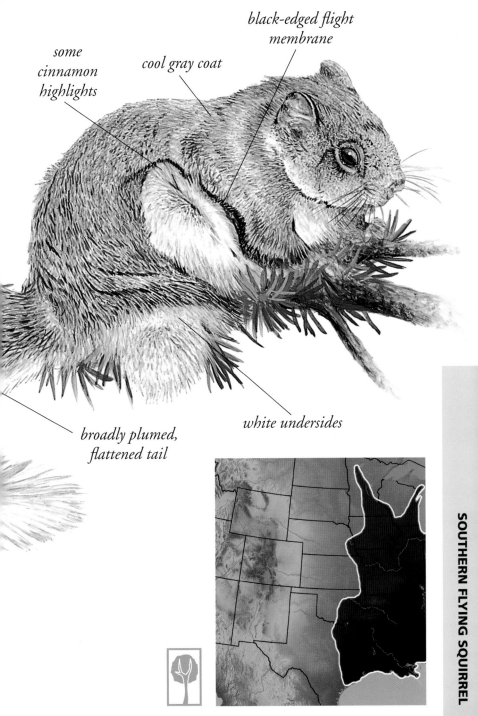

black-edged flight
membrane

some
cinnamon
highlights

cool gray coat

broadly plumed,
flattened tail

white undersides

SOUTHERN FLYING SQUIRREL

Northern Flying Squirrel

Glaucomys sabrinus

Like drifting leaves, Northern Flying Squirrels seem to float from tree to tree in the forests of Canada and some northern states. These arboreal performers are one of two species in North America that are capable of distance gliding. Enabling the squirrels to 'fly' are glide membranes—cape-like, furred skin that extends from their wrists to their ankles, down the length of the body. Before a glide, a squirrel identifies a target and maneuvers into the launch position, a head-down, tail-up orientation in the tree. Then, using its strong hindlegs, the squirrel propels itself into the air, arms and legs extended. Once airborne, it resembles a flying paper towel and can glide for up to 160 ft (49 m).

ID: smoky-gray to rust brown fur; light gray undersides; dark or dark-tipped tail; black-edged flight membranes.

Size: L 9³/₄–15 in (25–38 cm); Wt 3⁷/₈–8¹/₈ oz (110–230 g).

Habitat: old-growth coniferous or mixed forests.

Nesting: spherical, leafy tree nests; refurbished corvid nests; tree cavities.

Different from all other squirrel species in North America, both species of flying squirrels are nocturnal, favoring the twilight hours. The Northern Flying Squirrel and the Southern Flying Squirrel (p. 152) are not easily distinguished visually. The Southern Flying Squirrel is smaller and has a light, creamy colored underside, but the best way to tell them apart is by location.

The typical call of the Northern Flying Squirrel is a loud *chuck, chuck, chuck*, but it increases in pitch to a shrill falsetto when the squirrel is disturbed. Like the tree squirrels, such as the Red Squirrel (p. 146), which shares much of the same range, the Northern Flying Squirrel does not hibernate. On severely cold days, groups of 5 to 10 individuals can be found huddled in a nest to keep warm. Their nest structure is highly variable, ranging from abandoned woodpecker holes to refurbished nests of magpies, crows or other squirrel species. By late April or early May, the female bears three to six hairless, pink, blind babies.

SIMILAR SPECIES:
Southern Flying Squirrel (p. 152) is smaller and steel gray in color.

Southern Flying Squirrel

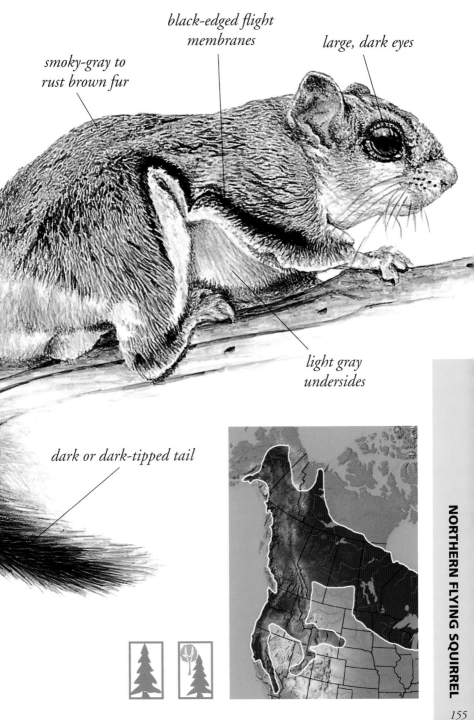

black-edged flight
membranes

large, dark eyes

smoky-gray to
rust brown fur

light gray
undersides

dark or dark-tipped tail

Glossary

arboreal: living in or pertaining to trees.

auxiliary burrow: an extra or escape burrow of an animal, separate from the home burrow.

bacular: pertaining to the penis bone.

cache: a store of food.

carnivorous: eating other animals.

colony: a group of individuals living together and interacting socially.

coniferous: needle and cone-bearing trees.

corvid: a member of the Corvidae family of birds, which includes jays, crows, magpies and ravens.

cranial: pertaining to the skull.

deciduous: trees that shed their leaves in fall.

diastema: a gap in the jaw caused by the absence of canine teeth between the incisors and the molars.

diurnal: active during the day.

dormancy: a state of inactivity, with greatly slowed metabolism, respiration and heart rate.

dorsal: pertaining to the back or spine.

drey: a spherical nest made of leaves, twigs and moss.

Red Squirrel

estivation: summer dormancy.

gestation: the time of pregnancy, from conception to birth.

herbaceous: plants lacking woody stems.

hibernation: winter dormancy.

hierarchy: a social order; the ranking of individuals by social status.

home burrow: the burrow in which an animal lives.

interbreed: when individuals of different species mate.

larder: a large store of food.

midden: a storage pile of conifer cones and seeds or a refuse pile of seed husks and cone debris on the ground.

migration: a movement of organisms from one area to another, usually in timing with the seasons.

morphology: the shape or form of something.

nocturnal: active at night.

omnivorous: eating both plants and animals.

pelage: the fur or hair of a mammal.

predator: an animal that preys on other animals.

propagation: reproduction.

respiration: the act of breathing.

subterranean: underground.

talus: scree or broken rock slopes.

torpor: a state of inactivity that resembles hibernation/estivation but is not as deep; heart rate and metabolism are slowed.

vibrissae: stiff and sensitive hairs growing on the face; whiskers.

Further Reading

Burt, William H., and Richard P. Grossenheider. 1980. *A Field Guide to the Mammals of North American North of Mexico*. Peterson Field Guides. Houghton Mifflin Co., Boston.

Jones, Clyde, Robert S. Hoffmann, Dale W. Rice, Robert J. Baker, Mark D. Engstrom, Robert D. Bradley, David J. Schmidly and Cheri A. Jones. 1997. Revised checklist of North American mammals north of Mexico. *Occasional Papers, Museum of Texas Tech University*, no. 173 (19 December 1997). WWW version retrieved 5 February 1999 from <http://www.nsrl.ttu.edu/opapers/op173.htm>.

Long, Kim. 1995. *Squirrels: A Wildlife Handbook*. Johnson Nature Series. Johnson Books, Boulder, Colorado.

Hole, Robert B., Jr. 1995. *A Checklist of the Mammals of the World: Rodentia 1 (Sciuromorpha)* [WWW page]. Retrieved 5 February 1999 from <http://www.interaktv.com/MAMMALS/Rodentia1sciur.html>.

MacClintock, Dorcas. 1970. *Squirrels of North America*. Nostrand Reinhold Co., New York.

Scotter, George W., and Tom J. Ulrich. 1995. *Mammals of the Canadian Rockies*. Fifth House, Saskatoon, Saskatchewan.

Whitaker, John O., Jr. 1996. *Field Guide to North American Mammals*. National Audubon Society. Alfred A. Knopf, New York.

Wishner, Lawrence. 1982. *Eastern Chipmunks*. Smithsonian Institution Press, Washington, D.C.

Woods, S. E., Jr. 1980. *The Squirrels of Canada*. National Museums of Canada, Ottawa.

Southern Flying Squirrel

Index

Page numbers in **boldface** type refer to the primary, illustrated species accounts.

With special thanks to Candace, for her guidance and inspiration,
and, of course, to Mom.—T.H.